"IF YOU COULD LOSE UP TO 20 POUNDS IN A WEEK WITH A DIET, WOULD YOU TRY IT?"

Of course you would.
And, now, here is the diet that could change your weight and your way of life.

FASTING:
THE ULTIMATE DIET

Start today, with your doctor's permission and under his supervision.

FASTING: THE ULTIMATE DIET

by
Allan Cott, M.D.

with Jerome Agel
and Eugene Boe

produced by Jerome Agel

(Abridged)

BANTAM BOOKS
TORONTO • NEW YORK • LONDON • SYDNEY • AUCKLAND

FASTING: THE ULTIMATE DIET
A Bantam Book / August 1975

2nd printing ... August 1975	12th printing ... October 1977
3rd printing . September 1975	13th printing ... January 1979
4th printing ... October 1975	14th printing . September 1979
5th printing ... October 1975	15th printing .... March 1980
6th printing .. February 1976	16th printing ..... April 1981
7th printing .... March 1976	17th printing .. February 1982
8th printing ..... June 1976	18th printing .... March 1982
9th printing ... October 1976	19th printing . September 1983
10th printing . December 1976	20th printing . November 1984
11th printing .. February 1977	21st printing ..... April 1986

ISBN 0-553-25967-9

Published simultaneously in the United States and Canada

Bantam Books are published by Bantam Books, Inc. Its trademark, consisting of the words "Bantam Books" and the por-
trayal of a rooster, is Registered in U.S. Patent and Trademark
Office and in other countries. Marca Registrada. Bantam
Books, Inc., 666 Fifth Avenue, New York, New York 10103.

PRINTED IN THE UNITED STATES OF AMERICA

H   30 29 28 27 26 25 24 23 22 21

Note

This book introduces to the public the concept of fasting as a regimen that has had beneficial effects, in cases described herein, for weight-reduction and for physical and mental problems.

Nothing in this book is intended to constitute medical treatment or advice of any nature. Moreover, as every person is adaptable to fasting in a different manner and degree, it is strongly emphasized that any person desiring to fast in even the least degree should, as for any diet, first consult his or her doctor, and should remain under the doctor's close medical supervision and advice throughout the fast and the entire period of adjustment thereafter.

—*Allan Cott*, M.D.

Contents

Fasting:
The Ultimate Diet

1.

Why Fast?

1. To lose weight the quickest and easiest way
2. To feel better physically and mentally
3. To look and feel younger
4. To save money
5. To give the whole system a rest
6. To clean out the body
7. To lower blood pressure and cholesterol levels
8. To cut down on smoking and drinking
9. To get more out of sex
10. To let the body heal itself
11. To relieve tension
12. To end dependence on drugs
13. To sleep better
14. To digest food better
15. To regulate bowels
16. To feel euphoric
17. To sharpen the senses
18. To quicken mental processes
19. To save time
20. To boost self-esteem
21. To learn better eating habits
22. To share with the hungry
23. To gain control of oneself
24. To seek spiritual revelations
25. To observe religious rites
26. To call attention to social issues
27. To slow the aging process

2.

All About Fasting

"I have found a perfect health, a new state of existence, a feeling of purity and happiness, something unknown to humans . . ."
—Novelist Upton Sinclair,
who fasted frequently.

"The ultimate diet."

That's what fasting has been called.

Understandably so.

When you fast—when you eat nothing at all—you lose weight the quickest possible way.

This fact has the support of an unassailable mathematical logic.

This fact also has empirical support.

You may lose four or five pounds on a one-day fast.

Or up to 10 pounds on a weekend fast.

Or up to 20 pounds on a week-long fast.

Extremely obese people may lose as much as 50 percent of their weight when they go on a succession of supervised fasts.

"Fasting is a valid experience," *The New England Journal of Medicine* reported. "It can benefit any otherwise healthy person whose calories now have the upper hand in his life."

The fasting diet is a reconstructive way of life.

People have been fasting almost as long as they have been eating.

Old and New Testament figures fasted. Moses and Jesus fasted for 40 days to bring on divine revelations.

The golden Greeks of antiquity fasted to purify their bodies and sharpen their mental processes.

In Russia, Tolstoy and his contemporaries fasted to divert the mind from materialistic concerns and to give the stomach a rest. (". . . to refuse food and drink . . . is more than a pleasure, it is the joy of the soul!")

British suffragettes fasted to publicize the inferior status of women.

American Indians fasted to induce visions and dreams and to placate their gods.

Colonial New Englanders fasted to save food and discipline themselves.

Fasting enjoyed great popularity in this country during the late 19th century. In those robust days people fasted simply to give themselves a "housecleaning."

Today Americans fast for all kinds of reasons—but especially to lose weight. Some of the other reasons are to:

- Feel better.
- Cope with soaring food prices.
- Cut down on smoking and drinking.
- Enjoy an "internal shower."
- Lower cholesterol and blood pressure levels.
- Acquire new—and better—eating habits.
- Attain spiritual "highs."
- Rid themselves of a junk-food past.
- Dramatize the plight of the starving.

Dr. Yuri Nikolayev, director of the fasting unit of the Moscow Psychiatric Institute, told me when I consulted with him in Moscow that fasts are *essential* for urban populations "constantly exposed to poisonous car exhausts, factory fumes, and other toxic air pollutants."

As a doctor who specializes in treating the mentally ill, I have used fasting as an effective measure in alleviating the symptoms of schizophrenia, which my distinguished colleague Dr. Humphry Osmond calls "the disease of the future." Many patients once given up for hopeless go on "miraculously"—after a period of fasting and the adoption of new dietary regimens—to live normal lives.

But for whatever reason people fast, they lose weight and feel much better.

When I lecture, I am often asked, "Is fasting safe?"

It is certainly safe for almost everybody. Each person is adaptable to fasting in a different manner and degree.

Unfortunately, we live in a culture that equates "three squares a day" with the preservation of life itself. It is mistakenly believed that to miss a single meal would be hazardous to one's health and well-being.

Actually, our body easily adapts itself to the fasting experience. It has ample resources to nourish itself for surprisingly long periods of time. The process of nutrition continues as though food were still being consumed. Fasting, notes a colleague, "hurriedly stops the intake of decomposition-toxins and gives the organism a chance to catch up with its work of excretion . . . it helps remove the toxins in the tissues . . . causes the body to consume its excess of fat . . ."

Fasting is *not* starving.

Starving begins only after the body's reserves have been exhausted.

Most people can fast safely for a month or longer. Our body gives the signal when it is time to end the fast.

It is a mistake to regard fasting as the panacea for whatever ails you. It is even a mistake to think of it as the cure for *anything*. But there is impressive documentation, such as Dr. Nikolayev's 30 years' experience with some 10,000 fasts, that fasting allows the body to mobilize its defense mechanisms against many ills. Healing is a biological process—as much a function of life as breathing.

Four hundred years before the birth of Christ, Hippocrates, "the first man of medicine," prescribed fasting as a measure to combat illnesses. "Everyone has a doctor in him," said Hippocrates. "We just have to help him in his work." ("To eat when you are sick," he also said, "is to feed your sickness.") Often taking his own "medicine," Hippocrates lived to the ripe old age of 90.

No one would dispute the wisdom of getting plenty of rest or taking an occasional vacation. Shouldn't we treat our digestive system to a rest now and then, too? Digesting food is the toughest job our body has to contend with. When we stop eating for a time, we give the system a chance to renew itself.

Hunger, amazingly, disappears during a fast. It may seem incredible that you can completely give up eating and not feel hungry, but there is a rational explanation. As long as you are eating anything at all, the palate is in a state of stimulation . . . savoring the last meal . . . anticipating the next one. When nothing is consumed, there is no "memory" of food to titillate the taste buds. Any "hunger pangs" are mild and ephemeral. Fasting is so easily tolerated because there is no sensation of feeling hungry after the second or third day. (Even the ultra-conservative *Journal of the American Medical Association* has reported this phenomenon.)

Fasting may be a healthier way to lose weight than any of the diets that restrict you to one food or to an unbalanced combination of foods. My post-fast diet— see pages 97–107—is designed to maintain weight-control.

I cannot stress this too strongly: *You should consult your doctor before beginning even a brief fast, just as you would before beginning any diet.* A long fast, even at home, must be done under the supervision and guidance of a doctor. It is best to undergo a long fast only in a medical setting. After any fast you should have a thorough medical checkup.

Too many of us live in a limbo where we feel just "so-so" or "okay." Fasting delineates the difference between feeling "just okay" and feeling abundantly alive.

I personally have never had a weight problem (I weigh about 138 pounds and I am 5′ 7″) and I always feel well. But when I fast for just a couple of days to feel really "on top of the world," I also lose four or five pounds.

Fasts are adaptable to a busy life. On a fast of a few days, there is no need to change your schedule. You can go to work. You can keep up with your social life. You should exercise, but don't jog. I recommend long brisk walks. (There's a saying among centenarians in the remote Ecuadorian village of Vilcabamba: Each of us has two "doctors"—the left leg and the right leg.)

People of all ages and from all backgrounds are now fasting: athletes, musicians, students, teachers, union leaders, clergymen, doctors, housewives, actors, construction workers, pharmacists, artists, designers, photographers, and "the working girl." We asked some of them to share their experiences with us. The following comments are excerpted from their "testimonials" (presented in chapter 15):

> "I am [now] a human dynamo."
> ". . . a new lease on life . . ."
> ". . . no more insomnia."
> ". . . I 'recycled' my body . . ."
> ". . . never lost weight so fast . . ."
> ". . . I experience a natural 'high.' "
> ". . . this bright new future."

Research for this book involved extensive travel. We visited several places around the world that provide supervised fasting (see chapter 26). We consulted with authorities in cities as far-flung as Buenos Aires, London, and San Antonio. In Moscow Dr. Nikolayev told me that treatment through fasting is "an internal operation without a scalpel," and William L. Esser, in Lake Worth, Florida, said that one should fast whenever one wants to feel better or look better.

Gael Greene, the biting (sic) restaurant critic of *New York* magazine, wrote us: "For a congenital gourmand, it seems easier and less painful to simply stop eating altogether rather than exercise moderation. The longest I've fasted was six days. Once for three, and now and then I fast for a day."

The vigorous actress Cloris Leachman, who sparkles as she describes herself as "sort of a mobile social worker," told CBS television viewers that she hates smoking and coffee and hard booze and sugar and meat, and that one of her solutions to the problems of the body is to fast. "Fasting is simply wonderful," she said. "It can do practically anything. It is a miracle cure. It cured my asthma."

You already fast every day of your life—between dinner and break-fast.

I hope this book will encourage you to extend your fast . . . to a full day or to a few days—or even longer.

Bon fast!

3.

It's a Discipline

Most diets are fads. They all hold out the promise of a rapid and painless shortcut to losing weight. Each has its season and is soon supplanted by the next "instant" fad to get rid of those unwanted pounds.

They come and they go:

The Mayo diet.

The grapefruit diet.

The Rockefeller diet.

The clamped-jaw diet.

The brown rice diet.

The hard-boiled egg diet.

The drinking man's diet.

The staple puncture diet.

The liquid 900-calorie-a-day diet.

The HCG-500-calorie clinic diet.

The 1000-calorie cider vinegar, lecithin, kelp, and B_6 diet.

Dr. Stillman's "quick weight loss" diet.

Dr. Atkins' "diet revolution."

And on. And on.

Senator George McGovern's Select Committee on Nutrition and Human Needs turned up no less than 51 egg and grapefruit diets.

Almost all fail. They are too restrictive and too monotonous to stick to.

In contrast to diets that are fervently embraced but soon forgotten, fasting is a discipline that has stood the test of time—*at least 5000 years.*

The thousands of people who are fasting these days

to lose weight rapidly discover that fasting, because it is *hunger-free,* is easier and pleasanter than being on a diet. Writing in *Playboy* magazine about his fasting experience, Malcolm Braly confessed: "I was grateful to have broken a lifelong obsession with eating."

4.

When You Fast:

You Lose Weight the Quickest Way

You are inevitably going to lose weight when you fast, even though losing weight may not be your goal.

In our weight-conscious society, however, more and more people are fasting *deliberately* to lose weight.

Is it any wonder?

We have learned from actuarial tables compiled by major insurance companies around the world that desirable weight for an adult is considerably less than average weight. The difference is about 10 pounds. One tends to live longer if one is thinner.

Some 80-million of us are overweight. More than 45-million of us can be officially classified as obese. At any given time at least 20-million of us are trying desperately to do something about our weight problem.

Annually, we spend billions of dollars to get rid of the excess baggage we carry around. We don't question the price if it's for some gadget or exotic dietary aid that promises the miracle of reducing and reshaping us overnight.

We hie ourselves to "fat farms" where the hospitality may cost a thousand dollars or more a week and where, after lots of exertion and sweating, we may drop only a couple of pounds. In the elusive quest we pay a pretty penny for supervised regimens and injections and suppressants and creams and powders and dietetic foods.

There are those who seem to make a career out of dieting. But can anything be more frustrating? All too often the lost weight "makes a comeback" when the diet is through.

When you fast, you lose weight at a rate that would seem to be impossible. You lose weight far out of proportion to your caloric deficit.

To lose one pound of fat you must burn up 3500 more calories than you consume. Most of us who lead sedentary lives do not burn up anywhere near 3500 calories *a day*. Therefore, it wouldn't seem possible to lose even one pound a day by consuming not so much as a single calorie.

But when you fast, it is not unusual to lose four or five pounds the first day and up to 10 pounds in two days.

The explanation for this equational discrepancy is quite simple:

Our bodies are mostly water. A 160-pound man is composed of about 100 pounds of water. (The rest of his weight is made up of 29 pounds of protein, 25 pounds of fat, five pounds of minerals, one pound of carbohydrates, and one-quarter ounce of vitamins.) Sodium in food causes water retention. As soon as you stop eating, *large* amounts of water are eliminated from the body. The scale does not distinguish between fat and water or bloat. A pound is a pound is a pound.

Stunning weight losses during the first days—far exceeding those of even Dr. Stillman's so-called "water diet" and Dr. Atkins' "diet revolution"—are a powerful inducement to continue the fast. My co-author Jerome Agel lost nearly eight pounds on the first day of his first fast—"it was fanfastic"—and he was not particularly overweight. (He told me later that during that fast he became aware of the hordes who eat in theatres, on television and even on the street.)

Contrary to what you may have been led to believe, calories *do* count. But in fasting there is nothing to count: no calories, no grams of protein, no grams of carbohydrates. And there is nothing to weigh.

Craig Claiborne, the esteemed food and restaurant critic, wrote in *The New York Times* of his week at the famous Montecatini Ferme in Italy where he went "to take the waters" and lose weight. He was put on a low-calorie diet that excluded fats, starches, all desserts except fruit, and all alcoholic beverages. He lost six pounds. Had he fasted, Mr. Claiborne might have lost three times that much. (A fast also leads to a more sensitive palate, which Mr. Claiborne would be the first to appreciate. He might also have found it *easier* to eat nothing at all. Low-caloric diets of 600 or 700 calories are not as tolerable as fasting: A little food awakens hunger without satisfying it.)

"How fast can I lose weight?"

The rate at which you lose weight is generally in proportion to the degree you are overweight.

Most overweight people who fast for a week can expect to lose up to 20 pounds.

Jane Howard, the best-selling author, told me that she lost 14 pounds in a week. Eugene Boe, a coauthor of this book, lost 16 pounds. Bub Redhill, a New York businessman, went from 242 to 222 pounds during his week-long fast.

(When he fasted for six days to protest Soviet treatment of political prisoners, the nuclear physicist Andrei Sakharov lost 17.6 pounds.)

Most overweight people who fast for two weeks can expect to lose at least 25 pounds. A 250-pound person can expect to lose between 30 and 40 pounds.

In a fast of four weeks or so, an overweight person can expect to lose about 20 percent of his original weight. A man who weighs 200 pounds on June 1, for example, can look forward to being 160 pounds by July 1. Harry Wills, the heavyweight boxer also known as the Brown Panther, a contender for Jack Dempsey's crown, would fast for one month each spring and lose *40 pounds* to reach fighting trim.

Extremely obese people have lost up to 50 percent of their weight in a series of supervised fasts. A 604-pound Chicago man lost 70 pounds in the first 10 days; through succeeding fasts, sensibly spaced, he lost more than 400 pounds. Another very obese man, who wanted to be "a human being again," fasted for 14 consecutive weekends. Then he fasted one day a week for nine months. Over the year's time he cut his weight exactly in half, going from 360 to 180 pounds.

At one time Dick Gregory weighed almost 300 pounds. He brought his weight down to 140 pounds through fasting.

British doctors are now using fasting for weight control. Dr. T. Lawlor, for example, has fasted patients for intractable obesity, at Botleys Park Hospital, Chertsey, Surrey. The patients ranged in age from 21 to 45 and were fasted up to 40 days. All of them tolerated the experience very well; a few even experienced euphoria.

At Glasgow's Ruchill Hospital researchers concluded that "total fasting is the most efficient method of reducing weight in obese patients." Dr. T. J. Thomson, a Scottish doctor who supervised the fast of a woman who lost 97 pounds through 35 weeks of fasting, observes that not only is fasting the best way to lose weight but that partial restriction of calories is ineffective.

You begin to live off your fat when fluid has been eliminated from your body. After the first heady days of the fast, the rate of weight loss naturally decreases. You slow down to a pound or two a day. But even the loss of a couple of pounds a day—following initial weight losses that are so dramatic—should be encouraging.

In the preparation of this book, my colleague Mr. Boe visited with Dr. Walter Lyon Bloom, whose pioneer work in the use of fasting to treat obesity was conducted at Piedmont Hospital in Atlanta. Dr. Bloom, now associate vice-president for academic affairs at Georgia Institute of Technology, came to fasting through his interest in fat mobilization.

In my research into obesity I found that fasting takes away the illogical idea that patients can't lose weight. My patients learned they were eating not because they were hungry. They learned they could go for a month without feeling famished. Fasting is probably the best self-disciplining practice I know. The only thing that counts in weight control is thermodynamics. It is pure, simple physics and chemistry. Weight is related primarily to balancing your energy intake with energy expenditure. Our preoccupation with eating at regular intervals has led to the misconception that fasting is not pleasurable. I have seen fasters lose as much as ten pounds in one day. What could be more gratifying, even though the loss is not fat but water.

As I said earlier, I enjoy fasting even though I am not trying to lose weight. By eating well—but in moderation—and by exercising I am able to maintain my weight and keep my waistline at 29 inches.

You may be interested to know what I eat.

For breakfast I have half a grapefruit or an orange, or the juice of either. I eat an egg twice a week and either a cooked or a granola-type cereal other mornings. I also have one butterless piece of toast with honey and a cup of decaffeinated coffee.

For lunch I have a cup of yogurt, or some nuts and figs or raisins.

For dinner I eat meat once a week and fish or fowl the other evenings. I always have a huge bowl of salad, with lots of vegetables, and usually a baked potato. In summer my dinner may consist of only a baked potato and cottage cheese and a huge Greek salad with oil and vinegar dressing. I almost never eat sweets. My dessert is a piece of cheese and an apple or a pear.

For exercise I walk a couple of miles every day, either to the office in the morning or to my home at night.

Let me stress my motto: "Less is better." And introduce a new one: "Let *them* eat cake."

President Ford asked Americans to cut down on food consumption by 5 percent. That amount is negligible, and hard to measure. But if we fasted one day a week we would be reducing our food consumption *by almost 15 percent*. Over a year's time this would add up to nearly two months of foodless days. Think of the savings in our food bills! Think how much weight we would lose!

You Feel Great

I have been blessed with good health all my life, but after a fast I am acutely aware of a sense of well-being.

My own experience is like that of so many others who observe that after even a few days of going without food they feel better physically, mentally and spiritually.

And now we are discovering what the animal kingdom has always known—fasting can be therapeutic.

Unless humans intervene, animals use nature's way to heal themselves. They find a quiet place to rest and they stop eating when they are ill. Even domesticated dogs and cats will resist strenuous efforts of worried masters to force them to eat.

So-called "dumb" cows are smart enough to quit eating when they are sick; sometimes they will keep their jaws clamped shut when cattle raisers or veterinarians try to force-feed them. Hunters have reported seeing a wounded elephant lean against a tree and watch his companions eat without joining them.

Man is the only "animal" who persists in eating when he is sick, even though he may have no appetite and food makes him nauseous. Though our ailing bodies reject food, we are still urged by everyone around us to "keep up your strength" or "build resistance"—keep eating, in other words.

The medical orthodoxy continues to take a jaundiced view of fasting, particularly as a therapeutic tool. This perplexed the late Alice Chase, who wrote on fasting for health: "The medical profession, ruling over the health of mankind, appears willing to subject the sick to the trial of all sorts of drugs, surgery, electric shock, and other forms of treatment that are experimental, even heroic—and sometimes useless. They are unwilling to open their minds and eyes to the more kindly procedures such as *rest of the body, mind and emotions*"—which fasting provides.

The orthodoxy opposes the treatment of the sick by non-medical practitioners. It has used its muscle to put many of these "healers" out of business. But under the supervision of naturopaths and hygienists many sick people have fasted and recovered from really serious ailments after their doctors had all but given up on them. Fasting and new eating habits were just what the doctor *hadn't* ordered.

But even when something appears to work, the profession is still not impressed. The "cure" has to be proved according to orthodox guidelines. Empirical data are not acceptable and scientific journals will not publish papers based on such data; the material is dismissed as "anecdotal."

To me it is even more regrettable that so many of my colleagues are not even interested in investigating something new that has been found to yield desirable results. But when the medical profession shifts gears from treating sickness to preventing sickness—and *it must!*—I have every confidence that fasting will be increasingly prescribed.

People who have chronically abused their bodies with too much food and the wrong kinds of food say that after their first fast they felt really well for the first time that they could remember.

Here again we can take a lesson from the animals. Many species—hedgehogs, bears, woodchucks, female polar bears—hibernate for months without a morsel of food. Birds and beasts of prey get along nicely without food for two weeks or longer. Dogs have fasted for 60 days. Fishes, turtles, and salamanders can go without food for even longer periods of time. But the record may be held by some species of reptiles; they can survive for a whole year without eating. (Tadpoles and caterpillars fast before they become frogs and butterflies.)

The incredibly energetic salmon takes no nourishment as it fights its way upstream to spawn. The journey may last for months and take it through 3000 miles of rapids and waterfalls.

In common with salmon, people discover they have amazing resources of energy during—*and after*—fasting. When we lose a lot of weight, we are naturally go-

ing to feel more energetic because our strength isn't being sapped carrying around all that "waste" poundage.

While fasting, Dick Gregory ran in the Boston Marathon. In England a man named Park Barner ran in the
52½-mile "double marathon," from London to Brighton, on a stomach that had been completely empty for
24 hours. "Not only did he finish without having his
energy run dry," the magazine *Runner's World* reported,
"he ran almost a half hour faster than his previous best
for 50 miles. Two weeks later, in a 36-miler, he used
the same fasting technique. He passed the marathon
mark within minutes of his best time at that distance,
and went on another ten miles at the same pace." In
the days when the University of Chicago had a football
team, Anton Carlson, the distinguished professor of
physiology, discovered that a fast of three or four days
before a game usually increased the energy and endurance of the players.

Dick Gregory has proposed a provocative idea for
the rehabilitation of prisoners, many of whom suffer
from malnutrition. "Prisoners who engage in purifying
fasts," he advocates, "could be credited with good-
behavior time. The penal system that initiates these
suggestions just might find it is on top of a tremendous
breakthrough in the area of rehabilitation. It just might
find that difficulties in rehabilitation stem more from the
jailhouse kitchen than from any other source."

Fasting is a calming experience. It is restful. It
relieves anxiety and tension. It is rarely depressing and
it is often downright exhilarating. A colleague at Mount
Sinai Hospital, in New York, tells us that fasting relaxes his muscle spasms, enabling him to reach a
plateau in yoga exercises that would otherwise have
been a long time in coming.

We have long ago discarded the myth of fat people
being jolly people. We know they didn't become fat
through just the joy of eating. Anxieties usually lead to
overeating, and it is the aftermath of overeating that
brings on fresh anxieties focused on health. Quick
weight loss from fasting can dissipate these anxieties.

I don't know just how it happens, but many fears

seem to disappear or diminish after fasting. I have
heard reports of people who lost their fears of flying
and crowds and darkness and heights.

One of my patients, who was a recent Harvard
graduate, had been a stutterer since he was three years
old; on the fifth day of my prescribed fast, his stutter-
ing stopped—and it has not recurred.

Nearly half the population (a staggering 100-million
of us) complain of sleeping problems. They sometimes
or always have trouble getting to and/or staying asleep.
During and after a fast many insomniacs discover they
are sleeping better than they have for years. This should
not be surprising. Fasting, which has been described as
"nature's tranquilizer," relaxes the nervous system and
eases the anxieties that account for much sleeplessness.
The internal organs are at rest, and this rest is conducive
to sleep. Much insomnia can be traced to the consequences of overeating or eating the wrong food:
heartburn, bloating, acid indigestion. Because the body
operates more efficiently during and after a fast, many
people find they do not *require* as much sleep as they
used to.

Fasting can be a cheap "high"—the cheapest "high."
A state of ketosis, difficult to distinguish from intoxication, can be reached. "Groovy" people refer to it as
"a trip," a drugless road to euphoria; they seek "good
vibes" and ecstatic visions. They also find that longer
fasts can bring on the desired state of susceptibility to
spiritual renewal. They flush out their systems and
break dope and junk-food "habits." (Their mentor,
Herman Hesse's Siddhartha, fasted.)

We are the most antiseptic people on Earth—exter-
nally. Others find excessive our germ-consciousness and
preoccupation with cleanliness. I wish we all were as
concerned with internal cleanliness. In a fast of a week
or so we can get rid of toxins that accumulate from
food we eat and the very air we breathe. It is a detoxifying strategy that gives the system "a clean bill of
health."

Cutting down on weight is one sure way to lower
blood pressure and cholesterol levels. A brief period of
fasting can bring down these levels dramatically. A

28-year-old-man, as one example, lowered his cholesterol level from 232 to 165 milligrams in the three weeks it took him to shed 35 of his 209 pounds. Follow-up fasts help to maintain the lowered levels.

Fasting may be effective in treating many more varieties of sickness than orthodox medical circles are ever likely to concede. I am dismayed by the number of my colleagues who brand all naturopaths and chiropractors and hygienists as "charlatans." On the other hand, I am also turned off by the extreme "naturalists," who claim the expertise of orthodox medicine is totally misguided. Both groups have something to contribute; they could be learning from each other.

All kinds of skin disorders are said to benefit from fasting. It isn't that fasting by itself cures acne or eczema or psoriasis. But the abstention from eating leads the way to a refeeding diet that can discover which foods or combinations of foods are causing the trouble. Skin irritations are often caused by habitual overeating, particularly of starches and sugars, or by some specific food or foods to which the person is sensitized. Many clear up after a cleansing fast and a new diet.

When I was in Moscow, I learned about the use of fasting in the treatment of venereal and dermatological diseases in the clinic of Lumumba University. At University Hospital in Lund, Sweden, researchers saw bald patients—both men and women—start to grow hair again after fasts of only ten days.

Sufferers from such assorted ailments as constipation, hay fever, asthma, peptic ulcers, arthritis, and colitis avow that their symptoms either disappeared or were greatly alleviated after a fast. I have read in the literature that "the value of the fast for the sufferer with hay fever and asthma is so fully established that we can only wonder why it is not more generally resorted to."

Interestingly, *Christian Century* magazine advised its readers to fast out of enlightened self-interest and not "the pieties of traditional Christianity." The objective was not to observe Lenten sacrifices but to lose weight, improve health, and make the body more vibrant and beautiful. "Fast because it is good for you," the magazine urged; it can be an "exercise to get the body in shape to be alive to itself. This process frees the self to be more sensitive to the Creation, to ourselves, and to our histories."

Roland Crahay, professor of psychology and sociology at Warocque-Mons Institute, in Belgium, has studied the psychology of fasting, and often quotes the credo of the famous Buchinger Clinics, in Germany and Spain:

> We must restore fasting to the place it occupied in an ancient hierarchy of values "above medicine." We must rediscover it and restore it to honor because it is a necessity. A beneficial fast of several weeks, as practiced in the earliest days of the Church, was to give strength, life, and health to the body and soul of all Christians who had the courage to practice it.

(The giant Chicago-based pharmaceutical firm Abbott Laboratories published the Buchinger credo in its house organ.)

In *The Great Escape,* "a source book of delights and pleasures for the mind and body," fasting is celebrated as "the ultimate diet . . . the only one that really works, not only for losing weight but for achieving a beautiful high and for getting a look into your cosmic consciousness. Try fasting."

You Look Younger

When you lose weight, you become younger-looking and more attractive. There is no quicker way to come by these desirable effects than through fasting.

Rejuvenation is both cosmetic and real. As the pounds come off, the streamlined reflection in the mirror lifts the spirit. You begin to feel and think younger and you move to a snappier beat.

We all know that we live in a society that reveres the cult of youth—and the desire to prolong youth. Fat is regarded as ugly because it is identified with age. An effective advertising slogan states: "You weigh ten years too much."

When I fast for only two days, lines in my face seem to go away. Many people report that, after a fast, their skin takes on a better color and texture; blotches and blemishes tend to disappear; it is almost like having acquired a fresher, *earlier* version of themselves.

"The skin becomes more youthful," says Herbert M. Shelton, who has fasted tens of thousands of people. "The eyes clear up and become brighter. One looks younger. The visible rejuvenation in the skin is matched by manifest evidences of similar but invisible rejuvenescence throughout the body."

In my opinion, regular fasts are far more conducive to rejuvenation than monkey- or goat-gland transplantations, hormone injections, face lifts, massive vitamin intakes, or any of the other extreme and expensive measures used "to turn back the clock."

The exterior *and* interior ravages of aging can be postponed if we periodically give our internal organs a rest and allow the body to eliminate or "burn off" its accumulations of rubbish. A more efficient metabolism acts as a rejuvenating agent.

In India a 76-year-old political dissident, Tara Singh, undertook a much publicized fast of 48 days. Afterward, examining physicians said it was their opinion that abstention from food had "increased Singh's life span by at least ten years." When he was on the tenth day of a fast, the illustrious Mohandas K. Gandhi, then 64 years old, was found physiologically to be as healthy as a man of 40.

An article in *Health* magazine stated unequivocally that if the average person were to fast one day out of every week for a whole year "he would be no older in body at the year's end than in the beginning."

On my second visit to Moscow, Dr. Nikolayev shared with me these personal comments on fasting by a man who had been fasting off and on for 50 years:

What do you think is the most important discovery in our century? The finding of dinosaur eggs in Mongolia? The radioactive watch? Television? Atomic energy? Hydrogen bombs? In my opinion the biggest discovery of our time is the ability to make one-self younger—physically, mentally, and spiritually—through rational fasting. With the help of fasting one can forget his age and thus prevent the processes of premature aging. I am 85 years old and proud of my agility. I can easily do yoga exercises standing on my head. Few people my age are able to do such exercises. I eat twice a day and never between meals. Every week I fast for 24 hours and three or four times a year for seven to ten days at a time. I believe a man can live for 120 years or more. Man does not use his common sense when it comes to food and drink and patterns of living; and then he dies too soon, not living even half his potential age. Even animals, if no one interferes, can live very long. Man is the only exception. Wild animals know how to live by instinct, what to eat and drink. But man eats the food that is most difficult to digest and drinks poisonous drinks. And then wonders why he cannot live for 100 years. In our mind we are all craving to live longer, but in practice unfortunately we are making our lives shorter. I consider physical weakness to be an insult to an instrument as marvelous as the human body. To be strong and healthy and to enjoy it—one has to work. A man can work miracles. But remember, only you can work for your health! You cannot buy it and nobody will give it to you. I am in perfect health and feel energetic all because I learned nature's laws and follow them. Fasting is the key to health; it purifies every cell in the body. I am sure that 99 percent of the sick people suffer because of improper nourishment. People simply do not understand that they litter the body by many unnatural foods, and—because of this—poisonous substances are collected in the body. If you are interested in being in good physical and mental health and in increasing vitality, start to work for this today *with nature,* not against her.

Paul C. Bragg, of California, a "life extension specialist," has fasted at least one day every week of his adult life. At the age of 85 he described himself as "a human dynamo," and was still climbing mountains. (Nine years later he is still going strong.) Mr. Bragg discovered early that even a two-day fast "will cleanse out an accumulation of toxic debris from your circulation system and vital organs so efficiently and effortlessly that you will promptly experience a powerful sense of rejuvenation of body and mind."

You Like Yourself More

Here are typical expressions of people who—by fasting—have learned they can be the master (rather than the slave) of their cravings. They reflect the return of self-esteem.

"I have never looked and felt so well in my whole life."

"It gives me a good feeling—no, it gives me a *great* feeling—to know that I am in control of myself, to know that I am no longer controlled by my appetites."

"I feel like a human being again."

A person in control of himself thinks well of himself.

Compulsive overeaters do not believe it is possible for anybody, let alone themselves, to get along without food. To them, the discovery that fasting is as easy as apple pie comes as a revelation. Self-regard, which may have been badly deflated, gets a healthy boost.

For cosmetic reasons alone, fasting is a boon to the self-image. It is much easier to like ourself when we are trim and our eyes sparkle and our skin is free of blemishes and our tongue is clean. The effects of fasting reach to the very center of our being.

Successful exertion of willpower gives us a keen sense of character-building. When we can say NO to a gratification that we have never resisted—especially to food and drink—we learn that we didn't know our own strength.

The first time most of us fast we make the amazing discovery that going without food doesn't "hurt" at all. Successive fasts become psychologically easier, too.

I believe there is enough asceticism in most of us that occasionally we get a good feeling out of denying ourself something. It gives us the chance to test our resources, to prove we need not be victims of our desires.

When we pass the test, we are entitled to reward ourself with at least a little pat on the back.

You Save Money

Most of us are aware of the health hazards and aesthetic liabilities of being overweight.

All of us are aware of the financial penalties.

In addition to all the money we spend striving to lose weight, the medical cost of becoming ill from afflictions and ailments directly traceable to overweight is already astronomical. And the cost of being sick for *any* reason may soon be out of sight.

The most economical way to get rid of excess weight is to fast.

A brief fast undertaken at home costs nothing at all. A supervised fast away from home costs only a fraction of a trip to a "fat farm"—and ensures much greater results.

You will save considerable money, as well as control your weight, if you make fasting a part of your life pattern. If you fast just one day a week, you cut your food bill by almost 15 percent (and there are continuing weight losses, another plus).

The average weekly "market basket" for feeding a family of four is going up up and away. In New York City in February 1975 the basket cost about $66. By eating nothing one day out of seven, a family of four could save over $9 a week, nearly $500 a year.

Just skipping dinner one night a week would cut more than 5 percent off your food budget.

The American Association for the Advancement of Science has predicted food-price increases of 20 to 30 percent a *year* for the remainder of the century. Not eating one or two days a week is the best way to absorb spiraling grocery bills.

During the present oil crisis we have been asked to turn down our thermostats to a healthful 68 degrees. If we choose to eat less on a day-to-day basis—or to eat nothing on some days—we would in effect be turning down our body thermostats a few degrees. By consuming less fuel (food) we also save money—and lots of it.

You Save Time

Another reward awaits you when you fast—the precious gift of found-time.

More of the day is spent in food-related activities than most of us have ever stopped to reckon.

The time it takes to eat "three squares" is the least of it.

Additional hours are also consumed in:
- Planning menus.
- Trips to the supermarket, butcher, greengrocer, baker, liquor store, and so on.
- Preparing meals.
- Setting the table.
- The cocktail hour.
- Clearing away dishes.
- Washing dishes.
- Taking out the garbage.
- Coping with food budgets.
- Anguishing over bills.

The average homemaker spends up to six hours—one quarter of the entire day—in the securing, preparing, eating, and disposing of food.

We are always saying we'd love to do this or to do that if we only had the time. Think of all the things you could do with a windfall of time. This alone is an incentive to fast. Here is a fairly pedestrian list of things to do with found-time:
- Lie in bed all day.
- Read *War and Peace*.
- See friends.
- Visit art galleries.
- Plan a vacation with money saved by fasting.
- Sit in the backyard and watch the cumulus clouds float by.
- Hike.
- Read to the blind.

- Shop for smaller-sized clothing.
- Learn Tagalog.
- Grow day lilies.
- Call Goodwill Industries.
- Enroll in a karate class.
- Meditate.
- Write poetry.
- Prepare and send to the radio telescope in San Juan, Puerto Rico, a message for transmission to extraterrestrials.
- Balance the checkbook.
- Have fun with a pocket calculator.
- Finish a game of Monopoly.
- Knock off early from the office.
- Put color photography slides in chronological order.
- Write a book on fasting.

There are millions of other things that can be done with found-time. The possibilities are as boundless as the human imagination and fancy.

Even a "half-fast" effort leads to found-time. A book editor in New York City told us that "as the day progressed, I didn't miss the skipped breakfast and rich expense-account lunch. I got lots and lots of work done, felt more energetic (and virtuous) and really had more time than I'd thought existed. Alan Lakein was right on time: Fasting is a great time-saving time whose idea has come."

Time will tell.

You Enjoy Sex More

A question I'm often asked is, "Is sex okay during fasting?"

The answer is yes, yes—but maybe not a thousand times yes.

Dr. Alberto Cormillot, whose world-famed clinic in Buenos Aires specializes in fasting obese people, told me that many of his women patients experienced an increase in sexual desires and that they tell him they "do it better."

A man in California said on NBC that when he "got involved" in fasting "one of the biggest changes was the increase in sex drive."

Losing weight enhances physical attraction. As the pounds slip away, all kinds of energies increase. Many men and women say that fasting started them on a *vigorous* sex life. Some discovered that they are sexually desirable for the very first time in their lives.

There are reports that extended fasts are beneficial for infertility. Women who were sterile are said to have conceived and impotent men to have become virile.

Fasting seems to stimulate the power of reproduction in lower forms of life. Some animals give birth during hibernation, when they are of course fasting. The aphid is rejuvenated when it stops its gluttonous habits.

It may not be too far-fetched to speculate that abstaining from food can have a restorative effect on the sexual drives and powers of reproduction of human beings.

In any event, I have yet to hear even one adverse comment about the effects of fasting on sex.

You Smoke and Drink Less

You must give up smoking and drinking while you fast. Both habits interfere with the fasting process; besides, drinking and smoking and fasting simply do not mix!

Alcoholic beverages are high in caloric content, and the consumption of any calories goes counter to the definition of fasting, of course. To drink on an empty stomach that is going to stay empty for awhile could also make you very ill. *Very.*

Smoking pollutes the body, which is also counter to the definition of fasting.

Heavy drinkers and chain-smokers do not seem to experience the painful withdrawal symptoms common to people who try to quit "cold turkey" without the support of a fast.

The body cooperates with bans on nicotine and

alcohol and other addictive habits like drug-taking and coffee-drinking.

While fasting, you probably will not even miss cigarettes or cocktails. As the body becomes "purified," there seems to be a built-in resistance to start polluting it all over again.

A week of fasting has been known to "cure" four-pack-a-day smokers.

It is a joy to know that we can take a drink or leave it alone. One midwest college professor told me that after a week's fast she had reduced her alcoholic intake from six to two drinks a day, and even to no drinks at all on many days. A writer for *Town and Country,* Lorraine Dusky, says that her fasts led to "a drastic reduction on smoking, even though I hadn't planned to cut down."

Fasting has been described as "a salvation for the man or woman who wishes to break the shackles of the poisonous habits of alcohol and nicotine." There is a "case history" of a severely disturbed woman whose central nervous system was "a shambling wreck." Every day she smoked four packages of cigarettes and drank at least a fifth of whiskey and copious amounts of coffee and tea. She was an insomniac. She had no appetite. Her thoughts kept turning to suicide. After ten months of intermittent fasting, the woman developed into a cheerful, productive person with no yearning to return to the addictive habits that had compounded her miseries.

One former heavy drinker reported that fasting drove the "devils of my former diet from my own temple" and that his life had changed completely for the better. "About three months after my first fast," he said, "I had a sip of scotch and soda and the taste was repugnant. I then remembered how bad liquor tastes to most people the first time they try it. Folks say you have to 'cultivate a taste' for booze. Even though the body is saying 'No!', people keep trying until they get used to it."

It is possible that after an extended fast the body will not *accept* unphysiologic substances like alcoholic beverages, drugs, and cigarettes. Alcoholic consumption can even be fatal if it matches the prefasting level. (Dr. Nikolayev believes that the body *cannot* accept unphysiologic substances after a long fast.)

It is my conviction that fasting gives such a sense of well-being that it is a supreme opportunity to give up *all at once*—or at least modify—dependence on alcohol, tobacco, drugs, and pills.

You Learn New, Healthier Eating Habits

E. M. Forster, one of Britain's literary immortals, observed that food is one of the five main facts of life, "a link between the known and the forgotten." It was a marvel to him that we can go on "day after day putting an assortment of objects into a hole in our faces without becoming surprised or bored."

In the course of a year the average adult eats 120 pounds of sugar, 53 pounds of fats, 100 pounds of white flour, 14 pounds of white rice, 25 pounds of potatoes, and five pounds of ice cream.

There can be no arguing that many mouths function as litter baskets and garbage dumps.

"Offending foods" cause fatigue and depression in adults. They drive children "up the wall," causing or increasing hyperactivity and interfering with their ability to learn. The Senate Select Committee on Nutrition and Human Needs was told that if sugar were being proposed today as a new food additive, its "metabolic behavior . . . would undoubtedly lead to its being banned."

A fast of a week or longer is an education. We learn that we can survive without any food for a time and that when we do start eating again it takes much less food to satisfy us.

Even our palate "reforms." We lose our taste for the sweet and the fatty and the highly processed and the synthetic. Our taste runs more to fresh fruits, vegetables, nuts, cheese, poultry, and fish. Some people become confirmed vegetarians after a fast—the thought of eating meat again even offends their aesthetic sensibilities.

After a fast—if I may be permitted a relevant pun—our overindulged appetite goes the way of all flesh.

Fasting makes food assimilation more efficient. It may be that it takes fewer calories to sustain us afterward because of the increased permeability of cell membranes.

Only about a dozen medical schools in the United States have departments of nutrition. Yet so many of the complaints that patients bring to their doctors are attributable *directly* to diet and to overweight. What we learn about nutrition so often must come from self-education.

If the medical profession were really "tuned in" to nutrition, would the waiting rooms of doctors' offices be "sweetened" with bowls of caramels and candy corn and jawbreakers and lollipops and all-day suckers? Would the corridors and the recreation rooms of hospitals be lined with vending machines purveying chocolate bars, sugary and carbonated soft drinks, potato chips, and other junk foods containing preservatives, additives, artificial coloring—with practically no nutritional value? Would cigarettes be on sale? Apples and carrot sticks and sunflower seeds and raw nuts and raisins and toasted soybeans—*that will be the day* you find *them* there!

The cliché "we are what we eat" no longer refers only to our physical being; it refers to our mental health as well. The state of nutrition affects our behavior and our mood, and can affect our sanity. The need to relate advances in the nutritional sciences to the body of medicine will soon be realized. Until the present, neither medical education nor medical practice had kept abreast of these advances. Medical teaching and thinking adhered to the narrow focus of nutritional deficiency diseases and missed the importance of diet in the creation of an optimum molecular environment for the mind.

The best hope for long-term weight control is learning to align caloric intake with energy output. A fast is an effective control. If we lapse into weight-gaining ways again, we know we now have an agreeable way of checking ourselves. Fasting, as the *Journal of the*

American Medical Association has stated, provides "the most important attribute of all—a method of self-discipline which all obese [and I will add *all people*] need and which can be repeated with beneficial effect."

Must every social occasion be marked by eating and drinking? At a funeral we bury the dead, then hurry home for refreshments. We bring food—usually the wrong kind—to the sick abed who would be better off eating nothing, let alone cakes, cookies, and candies.

A big banquet puts us to sleep—before the speaker even has a chance to. Hospitality in many parts of the country means being invited to a heavy dinner, and two hours later being served substantial snacks.

"My God," one man who had been fasting told us, "I would never have believed it possible. But there I sat drinking water all through a 'dinner' party and I probably had a better time than anybody else there. For once I really listened to what was being said, and I wasn't talking through a haze of alcohol."

In the healthiest of all possible worlds, we would follow the wisdom of the animals and eat only when we are hungry instead of eating at fixed times of the day.

Custom and social convenience dictate the hours when we eat. If it is 7:00 A.M. or noon or 6:00 P.M., it must be time for breakfast, lunch, or dinner. Many of us automatically get "hungry" around those hours.

Responding only to our body's actual needs, we would have about the same feeding schedule as babies. We would eat as many as six "meals" a day, spaced at intervals of every three or four hours. Each would be a mini-meal.

If we allowed our children to be truly self-regulatory and self-autonomous about their bodily functions, they would grow up eating only when they were hungry, as they did in their infancy. But they soon learn they must accommodate themselves to their parents' regimen of eating.

Dr. Jean Mayer, the Harvard professor of nutrition, points out that "you can become very fat by eating just one percent more than you need every day. That extra slice of bread and butter in the morning is all it takes to add a whopping ten pounds or so in a year."

No profession is more weight-conscious than show business. To project a desirable image, actors know they must stay fashionably thin. Many of them either fast or "semi-fast." One day a week Edie Adams, as an example, gives up all food and drinks only tea. Every seventh day Van Johnson confines himself to fruit juice. Octogenarian Mae West squeezes (she would!) the juice from six oranges, three grapefruits, two lemons, and adds an equal amount of distilled water; she sips this health-bearing elixir through one day a week. (It probably explains why she still has musclemen "comin' up to see her sometime.") Lynn Redgrave, who starred as the fat friend in the funny Broadway play *My Fat Friend,* is svelte in real life—now. "I've been fat," Ms. Redgrave has said, "craving food all the time . . . and now I'm thin and believe me thin is really better. I try to postpone eating until the dinner hour." Eartha Kitt eats once a day, usually at 4 P.M. The brilliant actor Sterling ("Bodily Fluids") Hayden—*Dr. Strangelove, The Killing*—has reportedly fasted up to a month. The memory expert and erstwhile professional basketball great Ejrry Aclsu stays in shape by eating only once a day and running around a lot.

The Japanese Imperial Army soldiers who came out of the jungles of the Philippines and Guam after hiding for as long as 30 years were in better shape than their countrymen back home, many of whom had grown fat in affluence. One of the soldiers ate only minute meals the whole time he was hiding out. Examining doctors declared him to be in top physical shape.

During World War II the British, whose food supplies were stringently rationed, remained remarkably fit. When food shortages eased, there was a decline in the national health and an increasing incidence of ailments that had been almost nonexistent during the siege. The countries of northern Europe had to reduce their food consumption during the War—sugar became extinct—and a decline in heart disease was noted. In Norway wheat supplies were drastically reduced—a fact that may have contributed to the astounding decrease in the number of cases of schizophrenia reported.

From the time he was a child, Thomas A. Edison

was taught to eat "just enough." He always left the dining table a little bit hungry. When his wife followed the "less-is-better" example, she became more youthful-looking and often was mistaken for her daughter.

I would be the last to lay down any arbitrary rules about when and how much we should eat. But I will say that a fast can help you get back in touch with your *real* dietary needs . . . to appreciating the taste of real food . . . and to knowing how much of it you want and when you want it.

To skip breakfast and even lunch—to go on a mini-fast—contributes to a desirable caloric deficit. Fasting the whole day—skipping all three regular meals—hastens that caloric deficit. Caloric deficits equal weight losses.

5.

The Mentally Ill Improve

My experience with fasting mentally ill patients began in 1970 on my first visit to the Moscow Psychiatric Institute. I went there at the invitation of Dr. Yuri Nikolayev, the director of the fasting unit, who was the first to suggest that schizophrenia may be caused by a biochemical imbalance that can be corrected through the restorative powers of fasting and revised diet.

Dr. Nikolayev himself fasts several times a year in 10-to-15-day stretches. "I usually fast for prophylactic reasons," he told me. "I have fasted several times with a scientific purpose in view, to make an experiment. I always feel excellent when I fast. It is always a happy occasion and a rest for me."

Dr. Nikolayev is fond of quoting an old German proverb: "The illness that cannot be cured by fasting cannot be cured by anything else."

Fasting *per se* is not a "cure" for anything—and I can not repeat this too often—but we know that it permits the considerable healing powers of the body— and of the mind—to assert themselves. An epochal breakthrough in the treatment of schizophrenia came when Dr. Nikolayev discovered that his patients responded to the fasting treatment after all other forms of therapy had failed. The patients had been chronically ill and felt hopeless about the future. Most of them would never have functioned again. Some would have committed suicide. Many would have deteriorated and lived out the balance of their lives in the bleak back wards of a mental hospital. *Seventy percent of those*

*treated by fasting improved so remarkably that they
were able to resume an active life.*

I was particularly impressed with one of Dr. Nikolayev's successes. At the Institute there was a nuclear
scientist whose case was diagnosed as senile psychosis.
His memory had lapsed to the point where he could
not recall his own name. But after an extended fast his
memory was completely restored and he regained full
possession of his intellectual powers.

The 25-day fasting treatment for schizophrenics that
I instituted at New York's Gracie Square Hospital was
in accordance with procedures used in Moscow.

Many patients ask if they can keep on fasting after
the prescribed period. They improve so much they
want to be sure their new feeling of well-being is "for
keeps."

Briefly, I should like to describe one of my most
rewarding "case histories":

A Canadian who had heard about my work at the
hospital directed his 19-year-old son to me. The youth
had had a nervous breakdown and was terrified of people and objects. He could not think clearly or concentrate. He was not capable of study. He had dropped
out of the University of Toronto. He was given to
hallucinations and delusions. He retreated to his bed-
room. His was a classic case of schizophrenia.

Private psychotherapy and group psychotherapy were
undertaken in Toronto. Drugs were prescribed. Electric
shock treatment was tried. Nothing was effective. As
each form of treatment failed, his depression deepened
and his withdrawal from life became complete. He slept
away the days. He suffered from severe, crippling
fatigue. He was written off as a hopeless case.

I started him on the fasting program, and by the
fifth day phased out the heavy medication he had been
taking for several years. In the beginning he did not
have an easy time of it. Added to his many fears and
apprehensions in general was the fear he would not
survive the fast. Fortunately, he made one encouraging
discovery early—his appetite disappeared. Food privation was no longer a threat.

By the tenth day of his fast my patient began to have

what he described as "happy feelings." He said they were the first happy feelings he had experienced in years.

His periods of feeling well became successively longer. His fast lasted until real hunger returned, which was four weeks. He took easily to the refeeding diet.

Four years later this once "hopeless" youth still feels well and is functioning effectively. "My mind is no longer muddled," he wrote me recently, "and I feel human again."

When Dr. Nikolayev learned that I was writing this book, he asked that I share a few of his observations with my readers:

I have pondered the paths that the fasting therapy method should follow, and concluded there are two: prophylactic and curative.

Timely measures for the prevention of a disorder must be considered very important. Fasting therapy can play a key role in this aspect. Systematic short-term fasts can raise the body's reactivity and defensive forces, and they can achieve overall improvement in the patient's condition.

Because the environment is constantly polluting us, fasting is essential for the arrest of the development of various chronic disorders, for the preservation of the health of following generations, and for defense against premature aging.

Short-term fasting also helps to reduce the duration of mass infectious diseases, since the body's defensive powers are activated and they can more effectively fight the disease.

I should like to stress that the schizophrenic person must fast only in a medical setting.

6.

"Our Finest Hour"

"Why can't a technology clever enough to dream up a product with no nutritional value [Coca-Cola] find a way to get milk to famished children in a land where the cattle have died of drought?"
—THE NEW YORKER

On the day the World Food Conference convened in Rome in 1974 and on the Thursday before Thanksgiving a few weeks later, about a quarter-of-a-million people fasted in the United States to underscore the plight of the millions facing hunger and death by starvation.

For most of them it was their initial experience with fasting. It gave them the feeling that it was in their power as individuals to do something to help the hundreds of millions who are threatened with extinction by famine. Moneys saved on food were sent to organizations responsible for getting emergency supplies to the hungry. We learned that we the overfed *could* share with the underfed.

The food exists now—but getting it from the lands of plenty to the famished takes money. In the future it will take money *and* a universal sense of sharing. "Our finest hour" is how a Washington Post Service writer described the possibility. "If misery remembers America in a kindly light," Colman McCarthy wrote at Christmastime 1974, "it will not be because its politicians wanted it as Number One—we were first in the number of bombs, cars, and can openers—but because we were the first nation in history to decide collectively to feed the hungry at a personal sacrifice. If we aren't remembered for that, all other glories will be forgotten."

Dr. Jean Mayer has astutely observed: "The same amount of food that is feeding 210-million Americans would feed 1.5-billion Chinese on an average Chinese diet." Nobody is hungry in China these days. Furthermore, the Chinese diet is considered to be one of the healthiest in the world. In other words, it is conceivable that we could get along in good health on about *one-seventh* of the food we are now consuming if we too could muster the knack of making less go much further.

Ours is certainly the most meat-hungry society on Earth. Beefsteak is considered as much a part of our birthright as corn-on-the-cob. As the economies of western Europe and Japan boomed after World War II, the more affluent citizens also developed a taste for prime steaks. The amount of red meat a nation consumes has become an index of its prosperity.

Meat is man's most expensive and inefficient source of protein. "World reserves of food grains are just about exhausted," *The Sciences,* the magazine of the American Academy of Sciences, declared, "and we are living on current production . . . this is a precarious situation indeed . . . the ghost of Malthus has been raised again."

We all know the grim statistics. There are about 4-billion people on Earth. By the end of the century there are expected to be 7.3-billion. Of the 2.5-billion people living in the world's less developed countries, an estimated 60 percent are malnourished and 20 percent are believed to be starving.

Food production may never be able to keep pace with the increasing number of mouths to be fed. "We have just about run out of good land," Professor George Borgstrom of Michigan State University has pointed out, "and there are tremendous limitations of what we can do in the way of irrigation."

Noting that obesity is America's number one health defect, Senator Edward M. Kennedy said that while half-a-billion children are threatened with malnutrition or starvation, America "stands in ironic contrast as a land of the overindulged and excessively fed. In many ways the well-being of the overfed is as threatened as that of the undernourished."

Do we need all the protein we are consuming? Must we get *any* of our protein from red meat?

A recommendation from U.S. governmental health authorities is that men should have 56 grams of protein in their daily diet and women should have 46. Whatever amount of protein we need, we certainly do not have to be dependent on a daily consumption of chops and steaks.

Dr. John H. Knowles, president of the Rockefeller Foundation, has urged that the U.S. provide the leadership in a new ethic of austerity.

The reaction of so many people who fast as a moral gesture to the starving encourages me to believe that our eating habits will change; and any change toward austerity will be a change for the better. It's a double boon, of course—the person who fasts also benefits, and in many ways.

7.

How to Fast

Drink Only Water

Strictly speaking, you are not fasting if you consume anything except water.

Even though other beverages may be calorie-free, you are better off avoiding them.

Black coffee and tea stimulate the central nervous system at a time when you are trying to give your self a rest. (I know that some doctors, including Dr. S. Heyden, of Duke University Medical Center, who has supervised the fasts of 2000 obese people, permit drinking of coffee or tea during the short fast. But as long as you're fasting for even a day, why not give the nervous system a complete rest?)

Artificially colored, flavored, and sweetened "no-cal" drinks recall the memory of food and may arouse hunger. At the same time they "poison" the digestive system and inhibit the purifying process.

Water is a faster's best friend. It facilitates the flushing of toxins and waste materials that accumulate when fatty tissue is being "burned." It keeps the body from becoming dehydrated. It also relieves those "hunger pangs" that sometimes occur at the beginning of a fast.

Man can stay alive for an astonishingly long period of time without food, providing he has water. Cloris Leachman told me that she thinks of water as "the fountain of youth."

I advise that you drink at least two quarts of water every day of the fast, but there is no limit to the amount of water you may drink. (There is the extreme example of a 428-pound man who drank at least five quarts of water every day while fasting.)

"If you drink two or more quarts of water a day, will some of the fluid be retained and show up on the scale as weight-gain?"

The answer is NO.

There is no reason for concern if you do not seem to be eliminating as much water as you take in. Much of the water you drink is eliminated through tens of millions of pores in your skin, which is the most dynamic organ in the elimination network.

It is best, at any time, to drink water that is not too cold. During a fast, drink mineral water if possible. Do not drink distilled water: It is the purest water you can drink, but its mineral content is zero. Ordinary tap water contains chlorine and fluorides—at the very least —and your palate at this time may find the taste of chemical additives especially offensive.

Many fasters treat themselves to an elegant goblet for their daily "diet" of two quarts of water, and they buy a case of Perrier mineral water.

During your fast you can be the life of the party as you move gingerly with your drink in hand—the ultimate watered-down drink—a glass of beautiful water.

Exercise

Contrary to popular belief, exercise does *not* stimulate appetite. An hour of exercise a day actually *reduces* appetite.

The body burns up calories faster, as we all know, when we exercise. But what is not generally known is that the body may continue to burn them up at an accelerated pace for as long as 24 hours *afterward*.

If the object of your fast is to lose weight, you will lose it that much more quickly by adhering to a daily exercise program.

I tell everybody who fasts under my supervision that

exercise is a must. I recommend brisk daily walks—up to three hours if at all possible. (And no pressing the nose against bakery or restaurant windows.)

During a fast of two or three days there is no reason why you cannot play golf or bowl or go bicycling—if that is your normal form of exercise. But you should not do anything as strenuous as long-distance running or jogging during your fast because they are sustained activities. Yes, I know that people do run in the Marathon while fasting, but I don't recommend it.

If you have been fasting for a week or longer, you may not wish to participate in activities with sudden movements.

Ease into It

I realize that most people do not consult their doctor before starting a fast, any more than they do before starting a diet.

But why not be on the safe side? Have a checkup before you fast.

The usual practice is just to start "doing it." A person makes up his mind that he is going to fast—and that's that, period. He wakes up one morning, skips break-fast —and the fast is launched.

Some people, however, need to "psych" themselves up. They "practice" by missing a meal or two for a couple of days. Or they feel they must indulge themselves in one homeric "last supper" on the eve of the fast. I certainly don't endorse a stuffing orgy, but if it takes one to *stop* eating it may be justified. It only means you start the "trip" with even more "baggage."

Take a positive approach. If it is your first fast, set your mind to experiencing it to the fullest. The average healthy person should have no apprehensions. Your attitude should be that you are going to enjoy it, as well as benefit from it—because you will.

New York magazine's sybaritic Gael Greene, who likes fasting, notes that though one experiences nobility, moral superiority and a pleasant euphoria in a long fast, "it does take a certain kind of motivation to psych yourself into the mood to fast." My advice is, if it's your first fast and you're wary: Try a one-day fast. It's a way of getting "the hang of it." A fast on a Monday after a weekend of partying works wonders—and will demonstrate how easy it all is. It gets even easier.

Start the fast with a purgative or laxative. It gives you a feeling of being "cleaned out" right away.

It is best to turn a cool ear to the warnings and dire predictions of your friends. The salubriousness of fasting is a concept still not universally embraced, in spite of its history.

Ignore observations such as "You look pale" or "You'll get sick." These are highly subjective comments, merely reflecting the fears of the people who express them. You may be cranky on the first day, but wait until you weigh yourself the next day! Watching yourself "scale down" each morning is so exhilarating that you will wonder why you ever hesitated.

Talk to people who have already fasted. Read the "testimonials" in chapter 15. The doctor who guides your fast will also be supportive.

Enjoy Your Normal Routine

A weight-loss program created by Dr. Heyden and the Duke University Medical Center has attracted much notice. It consists of fasting for 2½ days—preferably from Friday afternoon until break-fast Monday morning—and adhering to a 700-calorie-a-day diet during the work week. (The program is called the "Workingman's Diet" because it is tailored to suit the schedule, budget, and taste of the average working person.) A variation that results in even quicker weight losses is to alternate days of fasting and the 700-calorie diet.

On my second visit to the Moscow Psychiatric Institute I looked for a staff member I had become friendly with on my first visit two years earlier, in 1970. He didn't seem to be around. I finally asked for him.

I couldn't believe my eyes when the man was pointed out to me. He had been obese at our first meeting. Now he looked like a different man entirely. He was on the

25th day of a fast. Throughout the fast he had continued his full work load, and he told me he never felt better.

There is no reason for you to alter your routine, either. Your body will tell you if you're overdoing it.

As wastes are eliminated and body tones develop, you may find that you have increased resources of energy; you certainly should feel more vigorous than you do when you eat three substantial meals a day. And there's that good old proverb to ponder: "A full stomach does not like to think."

But a word of caution again: You should be careful of sudden movements, like jumping for joy or getting quickly out of bed. Quick losses of weight reduce blood-pressure levels; with fast, jerky motions this change can produce dizziness.

Do It With Others

Fasting loves company.

But not everybody is free to go to a retreat for fasting.

Fast, if you can, with your mate, lover, and/or friend so you can share the extra time meaningfully.

Join in friendly competition to see who is doing better on the scales.

Be mutually supportive.

Swap good feelings.

Stand in front of long mirrors, gazing in wonder.

Form a community fasting club.

Build a vacation around the fast.

Get lost in the great out-of-doors.

The rest is up to you.

Two of my "fast friends" had a contest when they first fasted together. They wrote down as many book, movie, play and song titles referring to "glorious food" (as it's called in *Oliver*) as they could think of. It's really amazing how many there are. Some examples: *Breakfast of Champions, A Clockwork Orange, A*

Moveable Feast, Jaws, Duck Soup, Dinner at Eight, Breakfast at Tiffany's, Tea and Sympathy, Top Banana, Milk and Honey, "The Candyman," "You're the Cream in My Coffee," "Life Is Just a Bowl of Cherries," "Little Lamb," "On the Good Ship Lollipop," Beethoven's "Fifth," "The Ladies Who Lunch," and *Grease.*

8.

Who's Fasting

Fasting is indeed an idea whose time has come.

Articles in mass circulation periodicals report that fasting "is a very good preparation for accepting a life-long program of low-calorie diet" and that it "is of great psychological value." Even women's magazines, whose revenues come largely from food advertisers, extol the virtues of fasting. Project FAST—Fight Against Starvation Today—sponsored by World Vision International —is a national endeavor.

As we were writing the last words of this book, our local media—the New York press—reported many fasting stories ... The National Conference of Catholic Bishops called for two days of fasting a week ... The country-western team Seals & Crofts were said to be celebrating a 19-day religious fast ... A woman in a much publicized court case (alienation of affections) revealed that she had fasted because "I had read that fasting makes you feel more composed." ... Bill Walton, the former U.C.L.A. basketball giant, told a *Sports Illustrated*-interviewer that he had fasted ... A poet working in a pilot writing program in Florida prisons said, on the second day of his second fast within two weeks, that "while we are turning down the thermostats, it would be a good idea to regulate the internal controls as well, to look within, to see what we have become." He wrote for the Op-Ed page of *The New York Times* that "a day of fasting, religiously observed once a week, would be a good place to begin." (Students at New York City's most prestigious high school, Stuyvesant, argued the poet's views in class.) . . . A Taft High School basketball player said that "I'm cutting down on eating. I go a whole day without eating and of course I never eat before a game. You gotta give the digestive system a rest." . . . Fasting was also "in the air." On an NBC television game show, "Blank Check," a contestant said that he had lost 40 pounds in 10 days—by fasting, of course . . . On "Masterpiece Theatre," a doctor prescribed a two-day fast for a sick woman in "Vienna 1900."

In increasing numbers young people have rediscovered fasting. They are fasting for at least three reasons:

1. To feel better.
2. To have "good vibes."
3. To express moral indignation.

They are now sophisticated about "empty calories" and drug addiction and food additives and alcohol. Forsaking food for a time is a way to "shape up."

Teen-aged girls are prompted to fast because they realize that chubbiness is not "in." All those cola drinks and chocolate cakes and pizzas!!! An article in *Playboy* magazine described a girl at the end of a long fast: "She just seemed to glow, she was transparently beautiful."

But may I urge that young people *never* fast, not even for a day, without their doctor's approval.

There used to be a consensus that children should not fast. But after extensive investigation, researchers at Duke University concluded that children can safely fast for one or two days a week *provided* that protein intake on all the other days *exceeds* the minimum requirement. In the post-fast diet you must be sure to get at least 60 grams of protein a day, as Dr. Heyden and his Duke colleagues discovered.

Some professional colleagues of mine—particularly Drs. Marshall Mandell, of Connecticut, and William Philpott, of Massachusetts—and I fast children with cerebral allergies in order to isolate the offending foods causing their disturbed behavior. We also fast adult schizophrenic and physically ill patients in order to isolate the offending foods that may be producing some of their intractable symptoms. Dr. Theron G. Randolph, of Chicago's Henrotin Hospital, reported to the twenty-third General Meeting of the Japanese Society of Allergology, in 1974, on successful fasts for physical conditions such as arthritis and ulcerative colitis.

It is not unusual for people in their 80s to fast, especially if they have been accustomed to fasting. When he was 85, Paul Bragg wrote *The Miracle of Fasting,* a book that has been an inspiration to thousands. When one fasts, Mr. Bragg wrote, one "lives in agelessness."

Herbert M. Shelton, who has fasted over 40,000 people at his "school" in Texas, wrote that "fasting can bring about a virtual rebirth, a revitalization of the organism." He suggests that "if we can see in fasting a means of enabling the body to free itself, not alone of its accumulated toxic load, but also of its burden of accumulated abnormal changes in its tissues, we can use this means of rejuvenation to great advantage. Recognizing its limitations and not expecting the impossible, we may still find in the fast an avenue perhaps not to eternal youth but to a protracted youth that endures long into what we once considered old age!" William L. Esser, who has directed a fasting center in Florida for several decades, himself fasts on a regular basis and today, in his "golden years," still plays a dynamic game of tennis. He is a glowing testimonial to the regimen he recommends.

9.

Four Illustrious Fasters

- Upton Sinclair.
- A genteel English housewife.
- Dick Gregory.
- Mohandas K. Gandhi.

These four fasted for quite different reasons. Their experiences are inspirational.

The novelist Upton Sinclair was looking "for a diet that permits me to overwork with impunity." He found it in fasting. Fasting so enriched Sinclair's long life—he lived to be 90—that he was frequently moved to rhapsodize about it:

> The first day I was extremely hungry. I felt the hunger pains that everyone suffering from dyspepsia knows well. On the second morning I felt significantly less hunger, and then, to my surprise, I no longer felt hungry. Before fasting I had headaches every day for two to three weeks. Upon starting fasting, I had a headache on the first day. I stayed out in the fresh air and warmed my body under the sun . . . The third and fourth days were the same: . . . a feeling of clarity in my brain. . . .
>
> I started to take long walks and write. But most of all I was surprised by the clarity and activity of my brain. I read and wrote much more than I could have before the fasting period. I slept well. Every day about noon I would begin to feel weak, but a massage and cold shower would restore my strength. . . .
>
> [On the seventh day of the fast] I have been about and busy every minute of the day and until late at night. I have walked miles every day and have felt no

weakness to speak of. I shall continue the fast until I feel hungry. . . .

On the 12th day I cut my fast short by drinking a glass of orange juice . . . My sensations afterward were just as interesting . . . I felt at peace and relaxed and every nerve in my brain felt like a cat taking a nap on a warm oven. My brain was more active than before, as proved by my increased reading and writing.

I had a desire to take part in physical work. Before the fasting period I went mountain climbing and walked distances only when it was necessary. Now I work out in the gym, doing exercises that before would have literally broken my back, and I do them with pleasure. I even feel the responsibility of becoming an athlete.

Before the fast I was very frail and weak; now I am strong and healthy . . . The fast is not an ordeal, it is a rest. I sometimes wonder if it is quite fair to call it "fasting" when a man is simply living upon an internal larder of fat. Above all else, it means that you must give up self-indulgent eating.

Mrs. Graham is a London housewife who discovered fasting when she was "a bit plumpish." She now fasts three and four times each year "to put my house in order."

In May 1974 she gave BBC audiences a day-by-day account of her latest fast. On the seventh day of the fast Mrs. Graham said that she genuinely regretted the thought of breaking it—she wanted to continue it another week—but she was giving a dinner party that evening and considered it poor form to be having only water while her guests were trying to eat, drink, and be merrie.

Mrs. G. decided to break the fast right on the air. She bid her audience adieu by biting into a very snappish apple. (There will always be an England.)

Dick Gregory has fasted in protest of moral, social, and political wrongs. He has found that "increased knowledge of proper diet has accompanied my deeper understanding of my vocation—participation in the struggle of human dignity." It was his idea that "a cleansing fast [was] needed by the American peace negotiators to see the truth about the Vietnam war from a clean, pure perspective."

When he appears in nightclubs and lecture halls and on college campuses and television, Gregory tells his audiences about the joy of fasting.

> One fasts for the purpose of cleaning out the system, eliminating all toxic poisons collected in the body. Fasting is detoxification of the body. It is based upon the conviction that toxemia is the basic *cause* of disease. When we continue to push food into the body, or to shoot chemicals into the body, as it seeks to heal itself, we are forcing the body to use vital energies for purposes other than the restoration of health. The best way to help the body when the symptoms of disease appear is through fasting, relieving the body of the digestive function, or taking only juices, which provide help in the process of healing. The long fast puts the entire body through a cleansing. The faster notices a heightening of ethical and spiritual awareness. There is an improvement of sex. The body requires less and less sleep because it is not involved in the constant process of exerting energy to digest food.

Gandhi, the most celebrated faster of this century, and patron saint of the modern peace movement, made headlines throughout the world by using the fast as a tactic in his non-violent campaign against British rule. He also would fast in penance for the "moral lapses" of his followers.

The Mahatma, once a barrister in South Africa, where he first fasted, was an ascetic. Since fasting can lead to heightened awareness, he felt it necessary to remind his followers that:

> . . . concupiscence of the mind cannot be rooted out simply. There is an intimate connection between the mind and the body, and the carnal mind always lusts for delicacies and luxuries. To obviate this tendency, dietetic restrictions and fasting would appear to be necessary. The carnal mind, instead of controlling the senses, becomes their slave, and therefore the body

always needs clean non-stimulating food and periodical fasting.

Fasting can help to curb animal passion only if it is undertaken with a view to self-restraint. Some of my friends have actually found their animal passion and palate stimulated as an after-effect of fasts. That is to say, fasting is futile unless it is accompanied by an incessant longing for self-restraint.

In the early 1930s Gandhi wrote about a recent fast in which there was "indescribable peace within." Observing that he had enjoyed peace during all of his fasts, "but never so much as in this one," he said there was:

> . . . undoubtedly faith that it must lead to purification of self and others and that workers would know that true Harijan service was impossible without inward purity . . .
> The fast was an uninterrupted 21-days' prayer whose effect I can feel now. I know now . . . there is no prayer without fasting . . . and that fasting relates not merely to the palate but to all sense organs . . . Thus, all fasting, if it is a spiritual act, is an intense prayer or a preparation for it. It is a yearning of the soul to merge in the divine essence.
> My last fast was intended to be such a preparation . . . How far I am in tune with the Infinite, I do not know. But I do know that the fast has made the passion for such a state intenser than ever.

(In India in the spring of 1975 protest fasts were being used by an 80-year-old Gandhian leader and his followers to win democratic rights.)

10.

No Reason to Be Afraid

"People don't realize that the chief obstacle to fasting is overcoming the cultural and social and psychological fears of going without food. These fears are ingrained."

—Dr. Charles Goodrich, Mount Sinai School of Medicine, New York City, who has fasted many times. (In taped conversation with Eugene Boe.)

At any suggestion to fast, some people still react with shock and indignation. Their wildest fears are instantly activated.

"A person would have to be out of his mind to fast," they exclaim. Or "Me fast? Are you serious? I don't want to die."

Many otherwise enlightened people equate fasting with starvation—and starvation with certain death. They believe it would be unhealthy to miss a single meal. But they can rationalize overeating on the theory that it lets the body store up reserves for some hypothetical "rainy day" when there will be no food to eat. What they seem not to realize is that *the body tolerates a fast far better than it does a feast.*

(Fear-inspired overeating can become a deeply ingrained, life-long compulsion—beginning in infancy and continuing often to an early grave. Frequently, it has its origin in memories of some *real* period of food privation—deep poverty or a famine or a prison or a concentration camp. One woman claimed that her obesity had its origin in the great famine in Russia in 1919. She was only a baby then, but she was stuffed with every scrap of food her mother could scrounge.)

The person who has allayed his own apprehensions about fasting may find that he still has to contend with the apprehensions of others around him.

Upton Sinclair wrote persuasively about this aspect of fasting:

> Anyone who has not read enough on the subject [of fasting] and who doesn't trust the method should not even start it.
>
> If possible, it should be done in the presence of a person who has fasted already. No aunts or cousins —no worry warts—who would constantly say that the person looks like death itself and that his pulse is below 30 should be present. Do not panic. Don't be anxious. I fasted for 30 days in California. On the third day I walked 15 miles and even though I had not rested I felt perfectly fine. Upon returning home, I read about an earthquake in Messina and how the survivors tore each other apart because they were so hungry. The newspapers in a fearful voice reported that the people went without food for 72 hours. I too lived without food for 72 hours. The only difference was that these people *thought* they were starving to death.

In September 1974, victims of a monstrous hurricane rioted in Honduras only a couple of days after they had run out of food. They probably rioted out of fear rather than out of real hunger.

If for any reason you have to go without food for awhile, keep in mind that the body is geared to sustain itself for long periods. *Nutrition is a constant function; it goes on whether or not we are eating.*

A graphic account of a plane crash in the snow-covered Andes is the subject of the best-selling book *Alive* by Piers Paul Read. A group of young Uruguayan athletes were en route to Chile when their pilot became disoriented and the plane hit a mountain. The survivors had an almost instant fear of starving to death. After only a couple of days their thoughts turned to cannibalizing their dead colleagues. Shortly thereafter, the thought became the deed.

The Donner party—a caravan of Midwest farmers emigrating to California in the 1840s—became snowbound in the Sierra Nevadas. Tension and frustration led to murder—and when food ran out, to cannibalism.

The experience of Ralph Flores and Helen Klaben, whose plane plunged into the wilds of northern British Columbia, in 1963, is in sharp contrast to these tales of cannibalism. Their "crash" diet consisted of a few biscuits and melted snow: hot, cold, and boiled. It was all they had for the entire seven weeks before rescue. When their ordeal was over, they were found to be in remarkably good condition, and both of course had lost much weight: he, 51 pounds; she, 45. (Ms. Klaben later said that she had been contemplating a diet, but a plane crash was not quite what she had had in mind.)

The writer Lorraine Dusky remembers that "when I first thought of going without food, the idea seemed impossible—but after having done it for two five-day stints I have turned into a zealot. Fasting brings a multitude of rewards."

Do not be concerned if you feel any unpleasantness at the beginning of the fast. Your body is undergoing beneficial changes. Side effects such as a slight headache, if they occur, are "healing" signs. They are momentary, and should be regarded as blessings in disguise. However, if at any time you find your fasting experience too unpleasant, consult your doctor; you may have to break the fast.

At the end of any fast you should feel much better than you did before you began it—and probably better than you have for a long, long time.

Please keep in mind that in fasting, as in so many other endeavors, *attitude* is vitally important. You stand to benefit most if you approach this wonderful new experience in a positive frame of mind. Put all fears behind you—they are inappropriate.

11.

Fasting Is *Not* Starving

The fact that the terms "fasting" and "starving" are frequently used interchangeably reflects widespread misunderstanding.

To repeat: Fasting is *not* starving.

Fasting is a positive, elective action that confers bountiful benefits.

Starving, in contrast, is usually an involuntary wasting away through the prolonged unavailability of food or adequate amounts of food.

The word "fast" derives from *faestan* (Old English: "to abstain"). The abstention is voluntary and undertaken for beneficial effects. It is life-enhancing.

The word "starvation" comes from the Old English *sterofan,* a derivation of the Teutonic verb *sterben,* which means "to die."

A person is fasting as long as he continues to eat nothing and experiences no *real* hunger. Starvation begins when the body has consumed its spare resources, craves food, and—for whatever reason—continues to be deprived of food.

Fasting and starving have only this *in common: Food is not being consumed.*

Again: Fasting is an act of will. Starving is an imposition of fate.

When we fast, we in effect decide we are going "to live off our self" for a time. We elect to take our nourishment from the "preserves" we have been "putting up" in good supply. Starvation occurs when "the pantry has been emptied."

Surprisingly, the confusion between fasting and starving is sometimes perpetuated by the medical profession and press. Too many doctors and science writers apparently still do not appreciate that to abstain from eating for a given time is not synonymous with starvation. But Dr. George F. Cahill, Jr., of the Harvard Medical School, has noted that "man's survival [of long abstentions from food] is predicated upon a remarkable ability to conserve the relatively limited body protein stores while utilizing fat as the primary energy-producing food."

It takes a long fast to cross the line into starvation. The body's acutely sensitive antennae will give the signal when it is time to break the fast, before starvation can begin. That time does not usually occur until at least the 25th day. The surest sign to start eating again is the return of spontaneous appetite.

12.

How Fasting Works

Nature takes good care of the body during a fast. Biochemical changes and "capital reserves" stored in the tissue combine to do the job.

In his classic *Man, the Unknown* the geneticist and Nobel Prize-winner Dr. Alexis Carrel defined the fasting process:

> Privation of food at first brings a sensation of hunger, occasionally some nervous stimulation . . . but it also determines certain hidden phenomena which are more important. The sugar of the liver and the fat of the subcutaneous deposits are mobilized, and also the proteins of the muscles and the glands. All the organs sacrifice their own substances in order to maintain blood, heart, and brain in a normal condition. Fasting purifies and profoundly modifies our tissues.

Fasting brings a welcome physiological rest for the digestive tract and the central nervous system. It normalizes metabolism. The kidney preserves potassium and sugar in the blood—an important element that assures our feeling of well-being.

Normally, the body constantly works to digest foods, eliminate wastes, fight diseases, ward off sickness, replenish worn-out cells, and nourish the blood. When there is no food to digest, it needs only a minimum of energy to carry on the other functions.

Here is, in medical terms, what happens during an extended fast of at least 25 days, based on my experience and documented by Dr. Nikolayev and his staff of biochemists:

Stage one—the first two or three days of fasting— is characterized by an initial hunger excitation. Conditioned and unconditioned secretory and vascular reflexes are sharply accentuated. The food-conditioned reflex leucocytosis is considerably increased and the electroencephalogram shows intensified electrical activity in all leads with a prevalence of fast rhythms. Excitative processes are increased and the processes of active inhibitions are relatively weakened.

Stage two—from the second or third day and extending up to two weeks—is a time of growing acidosis. It is characterized by increasing excitability of all systems concerned with nutrition and by hypoglycemia and general psychomotor depression. The person who is fasting loses his appetite, his tongue is coated with a light film, and his breath acquires the odor of acetone. Conditioned reflexes cannot be elicited, and unconditioned reflexes are greatly diminished. The food-conditioned reflex leucocytosis is sharply reduced. The EEG demonstrates a decrease in electrical activity. In this phase inhibition prevails over excitative processes. This reduction in excitation extends to the cortex and produces a state of inhibitions similar to passive sleep caused by the blocking of stimuli. Stage two ends abruptly in an acidotic "crisis."

Stage three begins when acidosis diminishes. The tongue gradually loses its white coating and the odor of acetone disappears. Unconditioned secretory and vascular reflexes remain diminished, and conditioned reflexes, including reflex leucocytosis, are absent. By the end of stage three, however, when the tongue is completely cleared and appetite is restored, secretory and vascular reflexes increase.

Fasting serves as a powerful stimulus to subsequent well-being. Acidosis provoked by fasting and its compensation reflects a mobilization of detoxifying defense mechanisms that probably play an important role in the neutralization of toxins. As the acidosis decreases, the blood sugar level rises. The pH of the blood remains constant after acidosis decreases. Other parameters of the blood continue to remain constant. Insulin levels become normal.

The biochemical dynamics during fasting are the same for healthy people and for ill people, including mentally ill people.

Controlled fasting, far from causing any irreversible alterations in the person's blood picture, stimulates a striking intensification of regenerative, and consequently of metabolic, processes. Research into the biochemical dynamics of the fast reveals the vast changes stimulated in all the systems of the body. The fasting therapy mobilizes the proteins in the body; this reaches a peak in seven days. When the recovery period begins, the protein level is found to be lower than at the beginning of the fast.

If a drop in glucose is to occur, as it occasionally does, it will happen between the third to 12th day of the fast and return to prefast levels by the 20th to 25th day. The glucose level returns to normal during the recovery period. If a person has hypoglycemia, his glucose tolerance curve should be normal at the end of the recovery period.

The hormone serotonin increases from the seventh to 15th day, and by the end of the fast the level is lower than it was in the prefasting period.

Histamine and heparin are both formed in the tissues that surround the blood vessels. During the fast large amounts of heparin are formed, which lowers the histamine level.

Albumin levels in the blood are not greatly changed during the fast.

Catecholamines in the urine of ill people are found to be lower than in normal people. During the fast an ill person's catecholamines increase and the level rises to that of the normal person. During the recovery period catecholamines increase above prefast levels. They are later maintained at normal levels.

13.

You Will *Not* Feel Hungry

Incredible as it seems, hunger may be completely absent during even an extended fast.

It is fairly common to experience "hunger pangs" at the beginning of a fast. They are a misnomer for gastric contractions or stomach spasms; the pangs are not the sign of true hunger, but the *sensation* of hunger.

It is the psychological or ritualistic aspect of eating that makes the very thought of fasting forbidding to many. *Feeling* hungry can be such a habit that the difference between "false appetite" and true hunger becomes indistinguishable.

Such "pangs" as might occur disappear after the first day or two of the fast. But on diets most people feel *constantly* hungry. As so many people have found out, it is far easier to sacrifice food altogether than to try to stick to a diet low in calories.

Studies at the University of Pennsylvania and at Piedmont Hospital in Atlanta revealed that fat people respond enthusiastically to fasting for a very simple reason: They experience no feelings of hunger. Many of them think they are "made differently" from normal people and that their weight problem is hopeless. Some are so elated by rapid weight loss—without discomfort and without a craving for food—that they plead to be allowed to go on fasting after the control period ends.

The scientific literature has reported the greater tolerance for fasting than for restrictive diets. "Fasting may be an easier way of losing weight," *Science Digest* said, "than [are the] extremely low-calorie diets." A letter to the *British Medical Journal* stated: "Fasting therapy . . . presents positive features . . . weight loss is quick, and, therefore, encouraging to a patient . . . hunger usually causes less discomfort than a diet and, at the refeeding, patients can easily tolerate an 800-calorie regimen."

How can it be, then, that you will be free of all feelings of hunger if you eat absolutely nothing for days—or for weeks?

When you eat anything at all, your gastric juices and digestive system remain in a state of stimulation. While you are still digesting the last food you ate, your palate is already looking forward to more food. When you eat nothing at all, your body steps up its production of a compound called ketones. These ketones, which are broken-down products of fatty acids, are released into the bloodstream. As they increase in quantity, they suppress the appetite. During a fast of about a month real hunger occurs when the body starts to consume its protein. The return of *hunger*—normal, natural, or instinctive hunger—is generally interpreted as a sign that it is time to begin the refeeding diet.

If you fast for a few days or for a week, you will not be truly hungry when you voluntarily break the fast. While it is pleasant to eat again—and food never tasted so good—you will feel that you could have continued your fast without discomfort. You know that it was *choice,* and not gnawing hunger, that caused you to terminate it.

Hunger is not cumulative. If you eschew food for a day or two or for five days or for even a month, you will not be penalized afterward by an insatiable appetite that won't be appeased until all those missed meals have been eaten. You will have appetite, but no feelings of being famished. You will find yourself eating more sensibly and selectively than before your fast. You *will* want to eat less—you *will* enjoy it more. You will agree that fasting is the greatest thing since sliced bread.

14.

Who Shouldn't Fast

Just as there are people who should never go on a diet, there are those who must *never* fast.

You must not fast if you have these conditions:

• Heart diseases, especially a predisposition to thrombosis
  • Tumors
  • Bleeding ulcers
  • Cancer
  • Blood diseases
  • Active pulmonary diseases
  • Diabetes (juvenile)
  • Gout
  • Liver diseases
  • Kidney diseases
  • Recent myocardial infarction
  • Cerebral diseases

Pregnant women have been known to fast, but under most circumstances I do not recommend it. Women who have just given birth must not fast.

Elderly people come through a fast with flying colors, but here again I would sound a note of caution. If you are in the senior-citizen category and have never fasted, you are advised to make *sure* you have the blessings of your doctor.

The very thin should not fast for more than a couple of days every few months, no matter their age. This is especially true of women, who tend to mobilize their scant supply of fat too quickly, with an effect similar to diabetic shock.

Do not fast without your doctor's approval if you are under his care for any reason.

15.

What It's Like to Fast

"But what's that for—the Great Fast? Why a fast—and why a Great Fast?"

"Because, Dyomusha, if you stuff your belly full it will pull you right down to the ground. You can't go on stuffing like that, you have to have a break sometimes."

"What's a break for?" Dyomka couldn't understand. He'd never had anything else but breaks.

"Breaks are to clear your head. You feel fresher on an empty stomach, haven't you noticed?"

—Alexander Solzhenitsyn

On the following pages (66–93) are first-person accounts, many contemporary, some historic, that describe the benefits and pleasures of fasting.

The accounts were contributed by people, of all ages and from diverse backgrounds, who fasted for a variety of reasons. (With the exception of the "case histories" with which I am personally acquainted, the following accounts are personal opinions and experiences without my corroboration, and must not be used as a guide to fasting.)

". . . a new lease on life . . ."

Since I've come to live in the United States, I have learned that the practice of fasting, despite its great antiquity, does not seem to have much respectability in the eyes of U.S. doctors, except for its quick weight-loss potential. Most doctors seem to view the human organism as an ailing machine in periodic need of replacement parts or chemical treatments.

I recently fasted at Buchinger Clinic, in Überlingen, Germany, to deal with a bothersome touch of arthritis, and because I needed a rest, and because it doesn't hurt anyone to lose weight now and then. After the fast, I was 12 pounds lighter, I had a new lease on life, and my blood pressure was lower. The bothersome touch of arthritis was also gone.

The idea of fasting is simple enough: Reduce the burden on the body for a period and it will start putting itself back into shape. Two weeks without food is the standard stretch, and it is—surprisingly enough—painless. When one stops eating, appetite vanishes. It was no problem to pass right by those tempting pastry shops in the nearby village and to limit myself to mineral water.

Alcohol and tobacco are forbidden during a fast. But it is surprising to see how unimportant such indulgences turn out to be and how easy they are to put aside.

Having just moved office and home, I'm ripe for another fast. I'd like to lose some more weight, and I could use another good rest. If I were like Voltaire, who treated himself to periodic fasts, I would fast at home. But I like the attention the clinic gives, and I like company.

> —Mrs. Jacqueline Nelson, senior vice-president, George Nelson Company, designers and planners. (In conversation with Jerome Agel.)

". . . excellent way to cure illnesses."

I got "hip" at age 29. I am now 73. Perhaps the four most important things I have learned during the past 44 years are:
—What to eat.
—When to eat.
—When NOT to eat.
—When to fast.

I am now a vegetarian. When I fast, to feel better or lose weight, I omit everything—all food, all juices except water. I prefer to drink spring or distilled water.

Up to age 29, and before I learned to eat properly, I was subject to colds, sore throats, stomach disturbances, and other common ailments. I learned to combat these problems by not eating and by going on a water fast. Fasting permits the digestive organs to rest while the bloodstream can concentrate on healing afflicted parts. Nature is always on our side if we only cooperate. My experience is not to eat when sick or in pain.

I fast until I feel better, usually one to four days. This regimen has been completely satisfactory for me.
—Samuel E. Sternberg, Chicago.
(In a letter to Jerome Agel.)

"I still feel like a new person."

My main reason for fasting was for health. I had discomfort because of a "faulty" gallbladder, and had some liver problems. After the first couple of days of fasting, I was no longer hungry. . . .

After the fast, I felt like a new person. The yellowish color of my skin and of my eyes had left, and there no longer was a gallbladder problem. I also lost 45 pounds on a frame that had been about 75 pounds overweight.

I am enjoying good health and watching carefully what I eat. I still feel like a new person. Fasting is a healthy and wonderful experience.
—Mrs. Ann Floyd, Libertyville, Ill. (In a letter to Jerome Agel.)

". . . music to my ears."

I'm on the road with my group a couple of weeks every month, and to tell the truth I become a junkie . . . that is, I can't stay out of those junk-food emporia. Burger this, pizza that. Convenient foods they are—convenient to bad health! Every time I return home I fast out those fast foods. Sometimes it takes three days to rid my system of the toxins. Fasting is music to my ears. No Jazz.

> —Flute player, Cambridge, Mass. (Told to Jerome Agel.)

"... I 'recycled' my body ..."

The first time I fasted I did it for political reasons. Two hundred of us were locked up together in the District of Columbia jail after May Day 1971. We fasted to protest high bail and various privations. Our youngest member, barely 18, told us how to conduct our fast and pointed out that it would have many physical benefits. Before long, the politics of the fast got lost in the body language of it. When I got out of jail I found that the celebratory roast beef tasted like Corfam and that I wanted to experiment with fasting and diets.

[When I moved to] a commune in the Santa Cruz mountains of California ... I "recycled" my body by means of a balanced vegetarian diet and regular fasts lasting from three days to a week at a time, once a month ... Now [my body] no longer accepts foods that do not suit its new condition ... my taste buds seem to have been totally transformed. Rice and vegetables taste better than a hot fudge sundae ever did. I eat a lot less than most Americans because my body uses food more effectively.

Experienced fasters claim that the average consumer utilizes only 35 percent of what he eats, whereas the recycled human can use up to 85 percent. I now fast mainly when I feel that I'm getting out of tune with my body or when I am injured.

Animals, of course, routinely fast when hurt, but I never connected that fact to my own experience until recently. I had sustained a couple of deep bone bruises that refused to get better over a three-week period. When I fasted, for other reasons, the injuries evaporated. I assume the body's building blocks could go to work on the injuries because they were not preoccupied with the digestive process.

—Sherman B. Chickering, teacher, political activist, San Francisco. (Reporting in *Harper's* magazine, and in letters to Jerome Agel.)

"I even like me better . . ."

Fasting is the flip side of my normal self.

I am overreaching, in some ways compulsive, previously given to overeating—and sometimes to smoking grass, which further stimulates the appetite.

Before I fasted, I often felt out of control with my eating. I was getting along, but on uncomfortable terms. Fasting is an affirmation of self-control. I prefer it to dieting because I prefer the feeling of not being hungry when not eating. If I eat just a little food, I'm hungry all day longggggg. My mind has properly convinced me that it doesn't matter if I don't eat—I feel and act better. I even like me better during the fast. And you will, too! As the bathing suit season approaches, fasting takes on added motivation.

—Phil Howort, theatrical agent. (Told to Jerome Agel.)

". . . now I can run fast . . ."

Three years ago I had a serious case of arthritis. Not a serious case in the chronic sense, but bad enough to hamper running. I couldn't sit down for more than half an hour without getting very stiff and I could not walk without a struggle for the first twenty paces. I went on a regime of careful eating of green and fresh vegetables and salads and two ten-day fasting periods in the course of eight weeks. And now I can run fast, as you probably saw in *The Sting*. Though age 64, I don't feel like a senior citizen.

—Robert Earl Jones, actor, New York City. (In a letter to Jerome Agel.)

". . . makes one proud of oneself . . ."

Having the discipline to fast creates a better feeling inside one's self, and the physical expulsion of body toxins makes the human being a stronger person. It is also true that if one fasts for more than three days, he or she will experience a "high" or lightness and lose the need for excess food or sleep. Fasting makes one proud of oneself for using his mind to control his body—something most people never use their will to control.

—Lynn Goldsmith, photographer. (In a letter to Jerome Agel.)

"Let me share a secret . . ."

For almost all of my 57 years—or at least since my fat childhood, when mother loaded me up with soup bowls of cereal every morning—I have tried what I think is every conceivable diet. Yes, including the Vomiting Diet —and me a fastidious lady! Not much worked, and nothing worked for long.

Recently, I had a brainstorm, which figures, for I've been for a quarter of a century a teacher and a principal in the New York City school system and I am now married to a doctor. In a flash I "figure"d it out.

Q. What made me gain weight? A. Food—swallowing it, anyway.
Q. How might it be possible to lose a lot of weight? A. Don't eat any food.

Q. What is abstinence from food called? A. Fasting.

And fasting is what I've been doing, and I love it and it loves me. It's the only diet that works. Lots of water, lots of urination, and a busy life. Let me share a secret: I feel more alive, even sexier, when I fast.

As a "foodaholic," I tend to overeat on weekends, but fasting beginning on Mondays brings me quickly back to a preferred weight and appearance. And I'm working on cutting down on weekends. But thanks to fasting, my tongue is more sensitive to food, making eating a great pleasure. I like people telling me how well I look, how trim I look, how gregarious I am.

> —Cynthia Kamen, New York City.
> (In conversation with Jerome Agel.)

". . . no more insomnia."

I went away to fast for a week and came back lighter by 14 pounds—the weight, according to my home postal scale, of three Manhattan telephone books. As soon as I got home, I rushed to my closet and preened before a full-length mirror in dresses that no longer felt as if they'd shrunk. (Before the fast, I had been inching toward outright obesity.)

Fasting taught me several things. I eat much less compulsively now, and more selectively. I have a new respect and sympathy for vegetarians.

Before the fast, I used to take meprobamates almost every night, either to fall asleep or to get back to sleep if I woke in the very early morning, as often happened. Now I don't even know where those pills are—it doesn't matter, because I have no more insomnia.

I also drink a lot less. In hedonistic New York it's quite usual to be offered, and accept, six drinks a day. Now I sometimes have none at all, and never a crashing hangover.

Fasting taught me how possible it is just to say "No thanks." I also learned, literally in my gut, that food need not be the obsessive concern our gluttonous society makes it seem. I keep meaning to fast again.

—Jane Howard, author, former *Life* magazine reporter. (In *Family Circle* magazine and in conversation with Jerome Agel.)

". . . extraordinary vibrancy and health."

My death sentence was pronounced by the doctor when I was 16 years old. A generally sickly body, heart symptoms, high blood pressure, profound anemia, and —perhaps most significant of all—a very heavy family history of early death from heart failure. All added credence to the stark prognosis made by one of Pittsburgh's most prominent physicians: "You have little chance of living beyond your early twenties."

I now wonder what was going on in his mind to make such a frightening prophecy to a 16-year-old. But he may have known something about reverse psychology, for my response was, "I'll show him, I'm going to live!" I did. I have.

I began to think about my system. I began to observe its reactions and to listen to its signals. Without benefit of guidance, I experimented with diet and with exercise. I noted carefully, when I felt sick, my diet and environmental factors, and I tried to note connections between conditions and feelings of well-being. I was on the path to self-awareness. Noting the clear relationship of our heavy Friday night Jewish East European meal with the terrible chest pains that inevitably followed, I began eating more simply, a lamb chop instead of chicken with fat lokshen soup, an orange or an apple instead of sugared cinnamon compote, a celery stalk instead of overboiled canned peas. Through my student days at the Curtis Institute of Music, my army stint, and my New York Philharmonic initiation, I began feeling better and better, even though I had reached the ill-fated "early twenties."

A fellow musician introduced me to "hygienic living" and to "fasting." I began an "eliminating" diet with occasional short fasts. For many months I ate only raw fruits and vegetables. The theory that the body quickly rebalances and heals itself, once it eliminates accumulated poisons, worked for me. My body became clean, strong, supple as I added fresh air, exercise, rest, and attention to emotional problems to the new diet. I felt marvelous.

During recent years I follow a less rigid and more varied regime, but I always "listen" to my body's needs and wants. I've added meditation to my daily exercise and to my diet. My friends, conventional or otherwise, will attest to my extraordinary vibrancy and health. I outrun, outwork, and outplay many people half my age. I love and enjoy life—and I am in my 40s.

—Joseph Eger, New York City.
(In a letter to Jerome Agel.)

"... made an important discovery ..."

As a seasoned member of the "yo-yo syndrome set," I have probably tried every diet. And I do mean *every,* good for me or not, crash to craze. It was inevitable that one day I would even try the fasting diet.

I learned through a little ad in *Prevention* magazine of Villa Vegetariana, a spa in the village of Santa Maria, just outside of Cuernavaca, in Mexico. I had been a vegetarian in my youth, following the example of my parents, who were influenced by the Shavians. I went to Villa Vegetariana with the thought that it wouldn't be much of a hardship to give vegetarianism another whirl with all those luscious and exotic Mexican fruits and vegetables to munch on.

The owner, a fruitarian by the name of David Stry, suggested that I might first try and enjoy fasting. I met a guest who was fasting and enjoying it, and I read Dr.

Shelton's book *Fasting Can Save Your Life*. I decided to fast.

My decision involved finding someone on the staff with a good strong right arm to whack off the top of a coconut. Whenever I felt a hunger pang, I was allowed to sip coconut water through a straw. Coconut water is rich in minerals and its caloric content is negligible.

Although I had been advised not to be too active while fasting, I felt just fine and saw no reason to alter my habits. I did calisthenics. I swam in the pool. I led a yoga class. I joined in the folk dancing in the evening.

I felt no lessening of energy during the five days I fasted. I continued to engage in all the pleasant activities that, frankly, made me feel as though I were a kid back at summer camp. I had a sense of exhilaration from beginning to end. I continued to enjoy myself without any feeling of hunger or deprivation, consuming only the water from one coconut per day. I even allowed myself the restful and pleasant joy of lolling in a hammock at siesta time.

I lost eight pounds—more joy!—experienced a heightened appreciation of my surroundings and a real sense of discipline, and I made an important discovery I should like to share: *Fasting can be fun!*

> —Gail Benedict, radio commentator and public relations consultant. (In a letter to Eugene Boe.)

"I don't catch colds . . ."

I was a sick man for 20-odd years—and then, in 1960, I discovered fasting. I have enthusiastically fasted in the summer each year since then.

I used to have at least one cold a month. I don't catch colds any more. My ulcer has gone away.

My business is ladies' shoes. Until I started to fast, my business was not what I would have liked it to have been. I was angry at the world, testy with customers. I was much too fat. My soul was poisoned. Thanks to fasting, my disposition is much improved, my business is much improved, and, as I say, I feel and look much better. I owe my life to fasting.

I eat no lunches, and I do a tremendous amount of walking. For six months every year I am a very good boy—a 67-year-old very good boy now—which lasts me for my annual six-month binge.

In the summer of 1974 I fasted for nine days and lost 18 pounds; two months later I had maintained the loss.

> —Irving Krutoff, Brooklyn. (In conversation with and by note to Jerome Agel.)

". . . see women friends more as people . . ."

I have been consciously working at personal development. With the onset of a job as an engineering consultant for transportation systems, I have tried an occasional fast. Each time I felt very together, enjoyed challenging situations, became very innovative, and generally dug life.

I feel that "I am" when I fast. Also, something of a relief, I see my women friends more as people and less as sex objects. Sex has become less compulsive and more spontaneous, conscious, and pure. It feels right, better than ever, and honest.

When my body is cleansed by a fast, I feel more in touch with myself and stronger in terms of self-assertion and willpower.

I am planning to fast for increasingly longer periods of time and hopefully under ideal conditions—outdoors in sunlight and without the demands and pressures of the working situation.

I am six feet tall and now weigh 150 pounds—and feel a hundred times as together as I did when I was a strapping 210-pounder. I believe that my life, finally, is expanding in good directions. What more could anyone ask!

—Victor Blue, New York City.
(In a letter to Jerome Agel.)

". . . got firmly back on the track of light eating."

I weighed in at nine pounds, and it's been uphill for 43 years. I even gain weight while watching the sugarland scenes in *The Nutcracker* ballet. I've tried every diet and lost thousands of pounds.

This last summer I lost 25 pounds by skipping meals and eating lightly. So many people said that I looked so lovely that I really wanted to stay thin. But along came the long Thanksgiving weekend and—well, you've never seen such a food binge. (Or I hope you haven't.) All my new clothes began pulling in the wrong places and I had to reintroduce myself to recent acquaintances.

I decided I just *had* to try "the ultimate diet."

For 48 hours I ate nothing and drank lots and lots of water. I walked a lot. I even did the family laundry and—to really test my determination—made meals for my *always* hungry family. I was so busy I hardly noticed a slight nervous headache.

Fasting worked! I quickly lost six pounds and I got back firmly on the track of light eating. By week's end I was again where I wanted to be.

Now I know I can binge from time to time and quickly get back to a preferred weight.

—Toni Z. Burns, Staten Island, N.Y. (In a letter to Jerome Agel.)

". . . I experience a natural 'high.' "

I regard fasting as more a spiritual experience than a physical experience. I started fasting to rid my body of excess weight, but I quickly realized that the fast is beneficial, very, for the mind. Fasting helps me see more keenly, achieve new thoughts, intensify my feelings, and, after a few days without eating, I experience a natural "high." Fasting inspires a sense of inner discipline and a controlling head. Insight into suffering and happiness comes during the fast. I have fasted many times, from one day to six days. I first fasted to clear my body of too much food. I wanted to feel my bones, and I wanted a slender body, not one filled with weights. I fasted after months of travel around the world, wanting to cleanse myself of all I had witnessed.

I had a memorable fast on a near-deserted New Jersey island. The beach became a beautiful place. Lying in a lotus position, I let the Sun shine on my body. I could feel myself grow lighter. I meditated. As I got "into" myself, I had the feeling I could accomplish telepathic feats.

Once craving for food goes away, the mind and the leaner body seem to stop craving things that lead to negative emotions like envy *and* jealousy *and* greed *and* overriding ambition—all those things the mental health poster says: "pride, fear, and confusion."

Fasting leads to a fine, strange edge on the world. Remember that Siddhartha's only skill was "Wait and fast."

I'm still smiling.

—Janet Fine, student,
Columbia Graduate
School of Journal-
ism. (In a letter to
Jerome Agel.

"I am a human dynamo."

I know the great benefits I have received from fasting, and that goes for my whole family. Every week I take a 24-hour or a 36-hour fast. This I never miss! In addition, I fast from seven to ten days four times a year. Over the many years (I am 85 years old at this writing) that I have been following this schedule, I have kept myself in a superior state of health. I am a human dynamo. I get more living out of one day than the average person gets out of five. I have an unlimited amount of energy for work and play! I never get tired . . . sleepy, yes . . . but never do I get that worn-out, exhausted feeling.

. . . A great feeling of energy flowed over my body when [the pesticide] poison passed out of my body. The whites of my eyes were as clear as new snow—my body took on a pink glow—and energy surged through my body . . . I had been fasting for 19 days—yet I drove over to Pasadena, to Mount Wilson, which is 6000 feet high, and climbed the trail with absolutely no exertion. I ran most of the way down the winding trail . . . In my personal opinion, fasting is the only way to rid the body of commercial poisons found in our fruits and vegetables.

. . . By fasting, extrasensory instinct becomes very keen. The fast sharpens the mind . . . tunes you in with the gentle voice of nature. Fasting has made my inner mind alert. I know positively that my mind works sharper and better after each fast I take.

If you can fast for three to seven days, most of your troubles of food disagreeing with you will be over . . . Flesh is dumb. It has all kinds of cravings . . . but you must be the master. You must control the entire body with the mind.

—Paul C. Bragg, N.D., Ph.D., Sc.D., "life extension specialist," author of *The Miracle of Fasting.*

"... never lost weight so fast ..."

Cold turkey without the turkey—a horrible thought. I became overwhelmed by the moments that food succored me. A pizza at the height of an argument with my wife, Anne, probably saved our marriage. She didn't know that those long walks to cool off were revenge binges, a vendetta—against myself. In my case, it was the Mozzarella Weapon.

To survive a fast, I thought, would demand a house call from Charlton Heston. He would throw down another commandment: "Thou shalt not eat!" But I took the big step—or the big waddle, in my case—and went the way of all flesh, all the way to the Pawling Health Manor. It's a retreat, and I surrendered.

Throughout my first fast I kept uppermost in mind the advice of Robert Gross, who was supervising my fast: "Fifteen minutes at a time," to paraphrase the successful Alcoholics Anonymous slogan, "One day at a time." And it works.

"Don't project too far ahead," Dr. Gross also cautioned. "You can get hungry just thinking about getting hungry."

It was the homecoming that made it all pay off. "Daddy, what's happened? You're so thin!" What a thing to hear your daughter say, no matter how darling and cute she is, as one comes through the door after having been away only three days at the fat farm. I was hardly thin—I had lost ten pounds—but had I been *that* "gross"?

I've been on and off diets all my life, but I'd never lost weight so fast and so painlessly. I didn't have a hunger pang the whole time. I recommend fasting to everyone. Since that first fast, I have fasted several times. As an actor, it gives me a good feeling that I can be in control of myself and to know that the frustrations and anxieties of the actor's life, no matter how often he works, no matter how often he gets to perform, no matter how often he gets paid to do his thing, can be coped with in ways other than eating b-i-n-g-e-s.

During that first fast I found that it helped to keep busy. I took several projects along with me. Another distraction, but on my last day, alas, was an invitation to dalliance. I was attractive to someone besides dear darling fantastic Anne. What a revelation! I didn't do anything about it, but it was still nice to know. . . .

> —Jerry Stiller, of the comedy team Stiller and [Anne] Meara. (In conversation with Eugene Boe.)

"My fast is a beginning . . ."

My fasting calls for justice in this world where two-thirds of humanity live in utter poverty. I organized a student fasting protest to attract public attention to the serious problems in our world of poverty, of hunger, of oppressive economic structures—especially with regard to the estimated 6-million starving people in the drought-plagued heartland of Africa.

My fasting is a tool by which I can open the eyes of man, eyes that have been shut for so long to the shame and agony that grip the lives of too, too many people today. I wrote a poem about my experience:

My Fast and the Africans

My fast was meant to break the bonds of apathy; their starving breaks the bond of life and hastens death.
My fast brings headaches and slight dizziness; their starving brings a torment to the mortal body, a constant fire.
My fast can be broken; their starvation is unrelenting.
My fast may bring applause; their starving brings looks of horror and disgust.
My fast is self-imposed; their starving leaves them bewildered, victims of the worst cancer.

My fast smacks of pride; their starving is pregnant
with shame.
My fast is a hymn, a song; their starving is a funeral
dirge, a cry that shrieks of the grave.
My fast is a plea to men; their starving is no longer
a plea but a dying demand.
My fast is a beginning; their starving is an end.
> —Brian Koehler, student, St. John's
> University. (In a letter to Jerome
> Agel.)

"I remain free of lesions . . ."

A severe case of psoriasis, contracted when I was only
nine years old, encouraged my initial interest in fasting
and natural living. I had been given no hope for a cure,
even by eminent doctors. It was just one of those things
I'd have to learn to live with, I was told.

By the time I was into my teens I was suffering almost
intolerable social ostracism and emotional distress. I
was ready to grab at any thread of hope, however
fragile. Fasting was suggested, and I fasted for a few
days at a time. I gradually changed my diet to mostly
fruits and vegetables. Between the fasts and the revised
diet, my psoriasis came under control. I remain free
of lesions; no one would ever guess that I ever had had
a horrible disease. I have been a vegetarian (no flesh
foods whatsoever) for 30 of my 46 years. My husband
has been a vegetarian for the same amount of time,
and he is healthy and vigorous at the age of 62. Our
five children have been reared in the same discipline,
and they have grown up with frequent short fasts.
> —Joy Gross, wife of Robert Gross,
> director, Pawling Health Manor,
> Hyde Park, N.Y. (In a letter to
> Jerome Agel.)

"... I experienced the spiritual thing."

Fasting is a fabulous experience! Everybody should do it every three or four months. Or oftener. Just to get back into their head.

I was 16 years old when I had my first fast. I fasted 11 days. I guess I fasted because I wanted spiritual knowledge . . . I wanted to be free of materialistic things and get out of my body. (My friends and I used to talk about things like this when we were kids.) About the ninth day I experienced the spiritual thing. But it was after I stopped fasting that I just automatically started to "travel" when I slept . . . visiting from plane to plane, planet to planet. It's been a decade since that first fast and I'm still traveling to astral bodies, maybe every other night. Sometimes I remember the trip, sometimes I don't.

So much happened after the fast. It opened me up. I just evolved. I harnessed knowledge that was exposed to me. It gave me a different outlook on this Universe . . . on every being walking the face of this planet. It convinced me that I would have to keep trying for something I can only call "soul development," the nearest thing to perfection on this planet. It made me wish I could be completely non-materialistic. Can you blame me for looking forward to my next fast?
> —Michael Altamuro, hair stylist with Charles Alfieri, Inc., New York. (Told to Eugene Boe.)

"... a sort of rest for the people, too."

To me, it was a vacation . . . we estimated that 10,000 people came here during the [three-week] fast . . . I think the fast was a sort of rest for the people, too. You know? Oh, I could go on for days about the things

that happened in the fast that were really great! . . .
And the people learned more about Martin Luther
King and about Gandhi in that fast than if we had sat
them down for a whole year of lectures.

—Cesar E. Chavez, president, United
Farm Workers of America AFL-
CIO. (Reported by Peter Matthies-
sen in *The New Yorker*.)

It was for the farm workers' struggle that I fasted
[three times], and it is for that struggle that we ask
your help.

—Mr. Chavez. (In a letter to Jerome Agel.)

"I never saw fat go so fast."

It has been an amazing experience: the pleasure of seeing those pounds melt away. I never saw fat go so fast.

My heart was very full when I left the school and all it
has meant to thousands of guests who, like myself, went
there sick and unhappy and left with a feeling of regeneration and happiness. I do not have the tremors
anymore. If I keep on improving as I am doing, I'll soon
be back to the days of my youth. In fact, I have had a
few compliments from strangers who said, "You look
very pretty this morning," and were amazed that I was
almost 71.

The brain becomes wonderfully clear; the body grows
into a recognition of its own power; languor, disinclina-
tion to mental and physical work disappear, and one
enters upon his daily duties with a vim and energy and
a delight that betoken the possession of the perfect and
abounding health that is every man's birthright.

—Three guests, Shelton's Health School, San Antonio, Texas.

". . . this new bright future."

. . . I came to you a large 200 pounds, with a blood sugar of 385. I had spent years as a diabetic and also as an obese person, which made my personality and my home life very, very sad. With your help I have lost 80 pounds and my blood sugar is a normal count of 120. I have God and you to thank for giving me the strength to take five fasts. What a beautiful feeling it is to have this new bright future. Everyone has been sweet and kind to me. Being at your ranch has inspired me. It has been a wonderful "Garden of Paradise" and a great Family of Togetherness. This has made me continue to have faith and strength to stay here . . . My eyes are filled with tears; time is getting closer to be leaving soon to face a new and happy world. But the tears I shed today are tears of happiness because I have had the opportunity to come down here and be under your guidance and loving care. I am now able "to look straight ahead," and not back at the past years of those horrible days and nights. I [am] sitting on a great big beautiful cloud, on top of a rainbow.

—Guest, on eve of leaving, Esser's Hygienic Rest Ranch. (In note [shortened] to William L. Esser.)

". . . self-confident for the first time . . ."

This is the first time during a life-long battle with overeating that I have been able to lose weight without the aid of diet pills. Amphetamines have caused me serious side effects for many years. I had taken all sorts of treatments and seen countless doctors. I was even hospitalized last year. Nothing helped. Each time I regained more than I lost. Now I feel healthier than I can ever remember. I found energy I never knew I was capable of. I feel self-confident for the first time in my life, and I know I will never regain that weight. I arrived at the [Buenos Aires] clinic in a size 28½ pants suit. I have already shed practically 100 pounds and hope in two or three months to be wearing a glorious size 12!

—Chronic dieter. (Reported in *Town and Country*.)

". . . ladies' best beautifier . . ."

As director of a fasting center for many years, I have supervised the fasts of thousands of people, including Dick Gregory.

I fast periodically myself. There is hardly an individual alive who could not benefit from a professionally designed fast, for fasting has no peer as to the benefits it affords to physical, mental and spiritual health.

Fasting is the ladies' best beautifier—it brings grace, charm, poise; it normalizes female functions and reshapes the body contour. During a fast, the emotional, mental, and spiritual outlook experiences a glorious upsurge and becomes re-directed!

I am often asked, "Does fasting enhance male potency?" In many cases it has accomplished just that. Sexuality is not confined, solely, to the genital organs—the body functions as a whole. No matter how exquisitely spiritual and tender our feelings are, physical disabilities—such as glandular exhaustion, fatigue and lack of energy—can well alter the course. Fasting—with colon therapy and proper diet—can correct the problems and turn back the clock.

In addition to the cosmetical, psychological, and emotional advantages of a more "tuned" body—which fasting inspires—there is the exhilaration enjoyed by even those who do not have a weight problem. There is also the "weighty" problem that is created when job and income are threatened due to the basic requirements of certain occupations. Airline stewardesses, models, actors, actresses and policemen, for example, have jobs that require regimented weight control.

When one goes into a fast, the body adjusts to new habits, correcting problems that cause constipation, high blood pressure, impotency, and the like. Men and women who reach 40 and over can be rejuvenated, and have more sex appeal.

I am often asked, "If fasting is so good, why isn't everyone doing it?"

My response: "That's just it—fasting is so simple and inexpensive no one believes it."

Controlled fasting is one of the safest, surest ways of losing weight, regaining health, and shedding a multiplicity of aches and pains, ills, and problems that stem from faulty eating habits of an over-indulgent nation. Fasting is the *perfect* way to natural perfection.

> —Alvenia M. Fulton, health consultant, Fultonia Health Food and Fasting Center, Chicago. (In a letter to Jerome Agel.)

"... felt peppier ... slept more soundly ..."

The most impressive finding [in my five-day fast, for weight reduction of course] was lack of fatigue and freedom from hunger after 48 hours. I actually felt sharper mentally, and was able to perform heavy surgical operations with skill and mental alertness equal to what I had when eating. A feeling of euphoria is noted by some people on a fast, and this was my experience. I actually felt peppier and more alert mentally. I slept more soundly than when eating regularly.

For spiritual uplift, try a fast. You will find that it draws you closer to God in prayer. It makes your character stronger by the self-discipline and humble experience of denying yourself food. The double benefit is your feeling of well-being, with a clearer eye, sharper brain, springier step, and greater efficiency for your work. It has often been said, "The man eager for success has the lean, hungry look." A bit of starvation can give you that eagerness in a hurry. Try a fast for spiritual and physical fitness.

—J. DeWitt Fox, M.D., L.M.C.C., editor, *Life and Health,* "the national health journal."

"... rejuvenation of the stomach ..."

... felt as if ... had had a month's vacation in the mountains. The mind was unusually clear and a greater amount of mental and physical work was accomplished without fatigue ... increased the vigor of the gastric hunger contractions to that of a young man of 20 to 25. The improvement or rejuvenation of the stomach is not a matter of subjective opinion, but a matter of objective record ...

—Professor Anton Carlson. (As reported by *Scientific American,* 1915.)

(Professor Carlson's five-day fast was reported by Maud DeWitt Pearl in the article "Hunger Strikes an Aid to Good Health." Ms. Pearl's conclusion: "The experiment settled any doubt as to the beneficial aspects of fasting ... Professor Carlson [well known at the time for work on the digestive system] had slept in his laboratory [at Chicago University] to facilitate record keeping; he continued to teach ... In the case of adult healthy persons, not only would they experience a general feeling of rejuvenescence but possibly the length of life might also be increased.")

"Life ... could be enjoyed, not just endured."

I became obsessed with the thought of food. I found that if I gave in to my fantasies to a certain extent, they actually helped me to feel more comfortable. Whenever I passed a restaurant, and there must be a million of them in New York when you are fasting, I would dream over the menu as though it were the gate to paradise. In my fantasies I gorged on pastrami sandwiches, ice cream, pizza, roast beef, chicken dinners, etc. Yet, at the same time, I felt that if I were actually face to face with a pastrami sandwich, I would not be able to eat it, and this was a very curious experience . . . After not eating for 22 days I had orange juice. It tasted like ambrosia. In fact, for quite some time after the fast I found my taste buds were very sensitive and food tasted so much better than ever before. Although it naturally took awhile to regain my physical strength, emotionally I felt better than I can remember ever feeling. Life really seemed like something that could be enjoyed, not just endured. The best part of it for me was the wonderful feeling of freedom. With schizophrenia I felt upset and depressed most of the time without even really knowing why. I felt driven by my emotions. My mind, instead of being able to judge the reality and validity of my emotional reaction, was just being driven by my feelings. Many times I wished I were dead . . . Now, even though I have some tangled emotions to deal with, my depressions are never as deep or as long; they are a response to real difficulties. Most of the time I feel well and able to work through the problems that come up. I cannot really express how good it feels.

> —Schizophrenic patient, who had been
> ill for 20 of her 41 years. (In a letter
> to Dr. Allan Cott after a fast.)

"My perspective is changing . . ."

. . . perhaps my major complaint of my illness was the feeling that my brain was not working right, not functioning spontaneously, that it was not, in fact, producing any thoughts at all. The only experience of thought I would have at such times would be my morbid brooding on my lack of thought. The clinical term for this is, I believe, poverty of ideation. This condition, I am much relieved to report, has apparently left me entirely, a fact I can attribute directly to my undergoing the fast.

There has also been an improvement in what might be termed socially related symptoms. My experiencing feelings of worthlessness when in contact with others has almost entirely subsided. I am much better at remembering and following conversations. Prefast, I would often become confused and be unable to engage intelligently in conversation.

Other complaints have also dissipated. My perspective is changing from that of a selfish child (shallow) to something much more mature and wise (deep). I am rarely depressed anymore. I believe myself to be still reaping the harvest of the fast. I liken it to a freight train gradually gaining momentum.

I experienced an incredible and wondrous sense of new birth. I became aware of myself as being a great quantity of human, emotional, raw material, which I can only liken to being re-made or reborn. I think this is a common feeling among fasters.

During the fast, my temperature and blood pressure were sub-average. Since the fast, I have been able to tolerate niacin at the rate of 2–3 grams per day with scarcely a hitch! Knock on wood. This may prove to be one of the most beneficial aspects of the fast. In the interests of life, I must do everything possible to improve my situation in all respects—organic, spiritual, psychological. As that great man Humphry Osmond would say, "No more mollycoddling."

> —Schizophrenic who fasted for 26 days. (Reporting to Dr. Allan Cott on a therapeutic fast.)

". . . I feel that I have a bright future . . ."

When I began to drink juice during the recovery period, the world changed. Colors became brighter and think-

ing became easier . . . I feel that I have a bright future
. . . I want to live a normal, healthy life, and I will
decide later whether I shall return to school.

> —27-year-old student from Poznan,
> Poland. (Interviewed in Moscow
> by Dr. Allan Cott.)

"I felt joy . . ."

I felt full of apathy. I was not concentrating, and when
reading I had to read a line over and over. When I
spoke to people, I could not remember what *I* had said.
I felt a complete weakness in my muscles. When in the
army I was punished by being isolated, I refused to eat
for three days—and found that I felt better. I decided
to fast or eat very little . . . the fast was terminated on
the 27th day . . . my appetite gradually returned, and
my spirits improved. I felt joy for the first time in a
long while.

> —Twenty-two-year-old schizo-
> phrenic patient. (Reported to
> Dr. Allan Cott at Moscow
> Psychiatric Institute.)

"The result was remarkable . . ."

During the time when I was a student in the medical
institute, I suffered from chronic nephritis and none of
the known European methods gave me any relief. Being
disillusioned in modern medicine, I decided to go to a
"school of fasting" and undergo fasting, in the city of
Fukuoka, where I was born. My parents were categori-
cally against it, but I went and fasted for eight days.
The result was remarkable: the albuminuria and
hematuria (from which I had suffered for many years)
disappeared completely. The unpleasant feelings, of
which I was so afraid before treatment, were much less
than I expected. The next year my father, who was

suffering chronic nephritis and hypertension, went to a school of fasting. Each of us fasted for ten days. As a result of treatment, I was cured completely: My father also noticed improvement. After being discharged from the institution, my father fasted every two to three months at home. His blood pressure lowered to almost normal. Albuminuria disappeared. From that time on my father was in good health and led an active life. I got acquainted with many other patients and kept in touch with them after treatment. Eighty percent of them told me in their letters about positive results, which convinced me once again about the effectiveness of this method. I began to advise everyone who suffered from chronic diseases to undergo the fasting treatment. I have cured with fasting patients with chronic diseases who had had no relief from drugs or injections.

> —Dr. Imamura Motoo, Japan. (Quoted by Dr. Yuri Nikolayev, Moscow Psychiatric Institute.)

"... lost 16 pounds in a week."

Before checking in at the Pawling Health Manor, in Hyde Park, New York, I tucked into a sumptuous last supper in the historic and picturesque Beekman Arms in nearby Rhinebeck and into a sumptuous buffet luncheon the next day at the same table. And then it was on to Pawling and "cold turkey" for the next seven days. I took to fasting like—well, like a duck to water.

I took long walks every day, usually to the neighboring village of Staatsburg. I became friendly with a librarian who had a "chocolate problem." I knew I had caught the hang of fasting when I could go to the general store and buy her a family-sized Hershey almond bar and not be tempted to take one wee nibble of it.

This was during a January thaw. Every day several of us gathered in a lean-to to take the mid-day winter Sun. But some of the conversation was not always conducive to keeping one's mind off food:

—"Where are you going to have your first meal when you get sprung from here?"

—"What's the name of that marvelous French restaurant on East 52nd?"

—"I can't wait to try that recipe for quick lasagna that I saw in *The News* this morning."

—"Did you hear that Shelley Winters got kicked out of here when she was caught sneaking in a pizza?"

I breezed through those waterlogged days feeling strong and chipper all the way. The most exhilarating moment of every day was the morning weigh-in. As a veteran dieter, hoping for a miracle from each year's new diet, I had never seen results like this. Or felt better. On my final trip to the scale that week I found I had lost 16 pounds.

I have now fasted four times, and I look forward to taking the fifth.

—Eugene Boe, a coauthor of this book.

"... can see poetry everywhere."

I first fasted on Yom Kippur, a traditional day of fasting, three years before my bar mitzvah. It was an ego trip to fast like the grownups. I fasted once a year for a few years, and then I went to pot—literally.

For about the next 15 years I led the opposite of a fasting kind of life. I finally weighed 260 pounds. I was a creature of consuming, not constricting.

I was sailing in the Greek Islands, with friends who had been to India and who meditated a lot and didn't eat often and often didn't eat at all. We talked about how Gandhi and Dick Gregory used the methodology of constriction for strength. That's how I came to fasting ... to find a controlling device ... to calm me down.

I fasted in France by a little river in a valley. I was surrounded by seven mountains. I had such an organic sense of life—Sun, river, mountains. I started to think of the people I loved, and I composed love letters to them.

Fasting is resisting the simplest of temptation. It is a tool that adds an appreciation of all things that are human and natural. A faster can see poetry everywhere. (The *Village Voice* reported that a cop on the vice squad who says he fasts one day a week protects prostitutes from being assaulted by pimps.) When life goes against me, I go to the eternally beautiful things. I fast and watch the Earth revolve in and out of sight of the Sun. Oh, Bucky, where are you?

Fasting teaches appreciation. And values. And respect. We are lucky. We have a choice.

—Max (Schwartz), poet, San Francisco.
(In conversation with Eugene Boe and Jerome Agel.)

Fasting
by Max (Schwartz)

Stuffing, stuffing, always they stuff, they stuff.
They grow fat stomachs.
They grow bayonets.
They grow rocket ships to the Moon.
But do they grow a simple caress?
Fasting.
What is the word fasting?
Fasting in truth is slowing
Slowing down of time
Putting time into one act of now
Putting time not into the out-there of random stupidity
Putting time into the appreciative cutting of the carrot,
The cutting of the celery, the cutting of the onion,
The serving of the tray, the giving of the glance,
The giving of the glass, the giving of the caress,
The simple time-felt being at one with the moment,
The simple time-felt, non-aggressive move to your crazy
    brother, who curses you.
You ain't got 30 bayonets
You ain't got swinging flashing fists
You ain't got all that speed.
You've just got a simple place of now
A simple place of appreciative being.
Don't rape the food, don't rape the bean.
You are the food, you are the bean
You are the beautiful pungence of the garlic
You are the slow simple sip of the tea.
You are the warmth of the teacup in the hand
You are the warmth of the tea leaves glowing
You are the warmth of the Sun
You are the simplicity of the Sun
You are the simplicity of the tree
You are the grandeur and simplicity of the Sun and the tree.
You simply can say a simple prayer,
You simply say to all, to everyone and everything that
    nourishes you:
Thank you.

16.

Easing Out of Your Fast

When you start to eat again, you will find that smaller portions are satisfying. A little bit of food can seem like a great sufficiency.

One of the happy results of fasting is bridling of appetite. There is no compulsion to compensate for all the food that wasn't eaten.

After a long fast the palate is restored to pristine purity. It prefers the taste of foods that are simple and whole and natural. It tends to reject processed and fragmented foods, as well as alcohol and tobacco.

There are a few general rules to observe immediately after the fast:

• Do not add salt to your food.

• Continue to drink a lot of water—a quart or more a day.

• Eat slowly and chew carefully. (This is always sound advice for anybody.)

We can benefit from Gandhi's vast experience with fasting. For breaking the long fast, Gandhi cautioned:

> I learned that a man emerging from a long fast should not be in a hurry to regain lost strength and should also put a curb on his appetite. More caution and perhaps more restraint are necessary in breaking a fast than in keeping it.

On breaking even a brief fast, it is important to be cautious about what you eat and how much you eat. To avoid overburdening the digestive system, only small amounts of food should be eaten at any time. Moslems semi-fast religiously—and unhealthily—for a month during the winter; they eat nothing during the day and gorge themselves at night. When I was in Tunisia in January 1975, I was consulted on ways my post-fast program could be introduced into the rites.

In my post-fast program I prescribe a diet that equals in length the number of days of the fast. It is also designed to maintain weight control.

17.

Eating Again

During the first day after your fast

In the morning mix two quarts of water with one quart of orange juice or apricot juice.

Sip two teaspoonfuls of the mixture every five or ten minutes in the first hour after breaking the fast. Sip teaspoonfuls at regular intervals throughout the day, but make sure the concoction lasts until bedtime.

During the second day after a fast of two days or longer

The diet consists of a quart of undiluted orange juice or undiluted apricot juice and at least one quart of water.

Drink four ounces of the juice at two-hour intervals. Drink the water in any amounts and whenever you wish.

(The new ingredient in the refeeding diet today is the undiluted fruit juice.)

During the third day after a fast of three days or longer

Drink one quart of undiluted orange juice or undiluted apricot juice—four ounces at a time at two-hour intervals.

Drink one quart of water in any amount and whenever you wish.

Mix one grated apple in two cups of plain yogurt. Divide the combination into five equal "meals." Have a meal every three hours.

(The addition to the diet today is the combination of the grated apple and the yogurt.)

During the fourth day after a fast of four days or longer

Drink one quart of undiluted orange juice or undiluted apricot juice—four ounces at a time at two-hour intervals.

Drink one quart of water in any amount and whenever you wish.

Mix one grated apple, one grated carrot, and two cups of plain yogurt. Divide the combination into five equal meals. Have a meal every three hours.

(The addition to the diet is the grated carrot.)

During the fifth day after a fast of five days or longer

Drink one quart of undiluted orange juice or undiluted apricot juice—four ounces at a time at two-hour intervals.

Drink one quart of water in any amount and whenever you wish.

Mix one grated apple, one grated carrot, one teaspoon of honey, one teaspoon of lemon juice, and two cups of plain yogurt. Divide the combination into five equal meals. Have a meal every three hours.

In addition, eat two slices of zwieback or melba toast, either with one of the meals or as a snack between meals.

(The additions to the diet today are honey, lemon juice, and either zwieback or melba toast.)

During the sixth day after a fast of six days or longer

Drink one quart of undiluted orange juice or undiluted apricot juice—four ounces at a time at two-hour intervals.

Drink one quart of water in any amount and whenever you wish.

Mix one grated apple, one grated carrot, one teaspoon of honey, one teaspoon of lemon juice, and two cups of plain yogurt. Divide the combination into *four* equal meals. Have a meal every *four* hours.

You may also have whenever you wish two slices of zwieback or melba toast and four ground walnuts.

(The new ingredients in the refeeding diet today are the four ground walnuts. Also, there are four meals instead of five.)

During the seventh day after a fast of seven days or longer

Drink one quart of undiluted orange juice or undiluted apricot juice—four ounces at a time at two-hour intervals.

Drink one quart of water in any amount and whenever you wish.

Mix one grated apple, one grated carrot, one teaspoon of honey, one teaspoon of lemon juice, and two cups of plain yogurt. Divide the combination into four equal meals. Have a meal every four hours.

You may also have whenever you wish two slices of zwieback or melba toast, four ground walnuts, a cup of cooked cereal with milk (do not add salt), and one slice of brown bread (pumpernickel).

(The additions to the diet today are the cereal and the brown bread.)

During the eighth, ninth, and tenth days after a fast of such lengths

The same as the seventh day.

During the eleventh day after a fast of eleven days or longer

Drink one quart of undiluted orange juice or undiluted apricot juice—four ounces at a time at two-hour intervals.

Drink one quart of water in any amount and whenever you wish.

Mix one grated apple, one grated carrot, one teaspoon of honey, one teaspoon of lemon juice, and two cups of plain yogurt. Divide the combination into four equal meals. Have a meal every four hours.

You may also have whenever you wish two slices of zwieback or melba toast, four ground walnuts, a serving of cooked cereal (a cup or less) with milk (do not add salt), and one slice of brown bread. In addition, at mealtime or between meals, you may have an eight-ounce serving of cottage cheese topped with a tablespoon of sour cream.

(The additions to the diet today are the cottage cheese and sour cream.)

During the twelfth day after a fast of twelve days or longer

Drink one quart of undiluted orange juice or undiluted apricot juice—four ounces at a time at two-hour intervals.

Drink one quart of water in any amount and whenever you wish.

Mix one grated apple, one grated carrot, one teaspoon of honey, one teaspoon of lemon juice, and two cups of plain yogurt. Divide the combination into four equal meals. Have a meal every four hours.

You may also have whenever you wish two slices of zwieback or melba toast, four ground walnuts, a serving of cooked cereal (a cup or less) with milk (do not add salt), one slice of brown bread, and one eight-ounce serving of cottage cheese topped with a tablespoon of sour cream.

In addition, you may have with one of your meals, or as a separate meal, two potatoes pureed with milk and one teaspoon of butter (but again no salt).

(The addition to the diet today is the pureed potatoes.)

If you fast beyond twelve days

Continue the regimen of the twelfth day for as many additional days as are necessary. For instance, if you fasted for seventeen days, you should adhere to the diet of the twelfth day for five more days.

When you go off the refeeding program, you may wish to initiate a diet based chiefly on vegetables, fruits, nuts and dairy products. The daily fare can be supplemented with a multiple vitamin tablet. Talk it over with your doctor. In any case, get adequate protein.

18.

Keeping Weight Off

"When I start eating again, won't I just gain back all the weight I lost?"

From my observations I would say that the chances are much better for permanent weight-control after fasting than after any diet whatsoever.

A posthospitalization questionnaire was sent to 709 obese individuals who had fasted at the University of Pennsylvania hospital, whose pioneer fasting program was supervised by Dr. Garfield G. Duncan. Of the 50 percent who responded, approximately 46 percent had continued to lose some weight, and 21 percent had remained at the reduced level at which they had completed their fast. In another study, Dr. E. J. Drenick, another fasting pioneer, in California, learned that 37 of 57 patients had continued to lose weight or to maintain their reduced level two years after a fast.

When anyone abstains totally from food, profound changes take place. These changes revise attitudes about food and put appetite into alignment with the body's real needs for energy.

After the fast, a few pounds may come back. This does not necessarily mean you are eating too much. The sodium content in food causes the body to retain fluid, which shows up as weight on the scales.

A fast of a day or two should correct any slight gains in weight, and in fact could lead to lower weight plateaus.

After the initial fast, the average woman can lose an

additional 1½ to 2½ pounds every week on a daily diet of 1300 to 1500 calories. The average man can lose the same amount with the more liberal daily ration of 1500 to 1900 calories.

19.

Fasting Again

"When can I fast again?"

You can always fast for one or two days a week.

Or you may prefer an occasional three-to-five-day fast.

If you have recently completed a fast of 25 days or longer, you should wait six months before repeating it, and then only in a medical setting of course.

Whether you fast a day or three days or five days at a time, the total in any month should not exceed 10 days *if you fast on a regular basis.*

You must never go below the minimum level of weight your doctor recommends.

20.

Longer Fasts

If you are fasting for a week or longer:
- Keep in touch with your doctor.
- Drink at least two quarts of water every day.
- Exercise as much as you can.
- Do not take medication or pills of any kind without your doctor's approval. (During a fast of a few days you may continue with vitamins and minerals.)
- Keep warm.
- Get plenty of fresh air.
- Rest out-of-doors if possible.
- Sunbathe in the morning when direct and prolonged exposure to the Sun is not as dangerous as later in the day (a sensible health measure at any time).
- Do not drink anything except water. No coffee, no tea, no diluted juices, no non-caloric soft drinks, and certainly no alcohol.
- Do not smoke.
- Shower or bathe frequently. (This is hygienically a good idea because the body rids itself of toxins through the skin. To stimulate the skin use a rough, pliable straw mitt as a wash cloth.)
- Avoid hot baths and saunas.
- Be careful of sudden movement; lowered blood pressure can make you dizzy.
- Do not take diuretics.

Opinion is mixed on the subject of car-driving during a long fast. Fasting can lead to euphoria, even to a slight sense of intoxication—conditions unfavorable to safe driving. I do not believe there is any rigid rule to be laid down on the subject. The best guide to whether you should drive is simply how you feel.

(Before starting a long fast, as before starting any long-term weight-reducing diet, it is advisable to have a medical examination that includes a liver profile and an electrocardiogram.)

The dos and don'ts of the longer fast—for best results—are also applicable to the shorter fast, of course; most of them make excellent sense even when you are not fasting.

21.

Breaking the Longer Fast

The return of appetite and the appearance of a clean tongue, fresh mouth odor, and clear urine are sure signs that you have completed your long fast and it is time to start eating again.

These manifestations usually appear around the 25th day of a long fast. They can appear earlier.

Certain symptoms indicate that metabolism is not functioning properly, and they, too, make it imperative for your doctor to end the fast. These symptoms include:

• Persistence of hunger beyond the fourth day (the reason could be an overabundance of insulin) or the unexpected reappearance of appetite.

• An abnormal cardiac rhythm or persistent rapid pulse beat.

• Gastric or intestinal spasm or symptoms of a surgical abdomen. (If the spasm is functional, medications can be given by a doctor and the fast continued.)

• Cardiac asthma.

• Prolonged periods of nausea or vomiting, headaches, dizziness, or weakness.

• A marked fall in plasma and extracellular fluid volume, resulting in varying degrees of postural hypotension. (Your doctor can retard fluid loss with a daily gram of bicarbonate of soda.)

Your doctor may advise you that there is no need to break the fast if you catch a cold or get an upper respiratory infection. In fact, you might get rid of such an illness quicker if you stay on the fast.

22.

Side Effects Can Be Healthy Signs

At the beginning of a fast you may experience some unpleasant side effects such as headaches, nausea, or dizziness.

These should be no cause for alarm or discouragement. They are usually transitory. If they do not disappear after a couple of days, consult your doctor.

These effects are, in fact, healthy signs. They are indications that the body is ridding itself of waste materials. They are a step on the way to feeling really well both physically and mentally.

Do not worry if there *isn't* even a moment of unpleasantness or discomfort; the purification of the system is still going on. I have rarely had a nauseous patient, though nausea is considered normal in the "getting better" process.

A great many people sail through even lengthy fasts without feeling a moment of discomfort. I have never had a moment of discomfort; my coauthor Eugene Boe has fasted frequently and for varying lengths of time and has never had a moment of discomfort. *Attitude does help*.

Gnawing in the stomach is common on the first two to three days of a fast. Remember: It is not a hunger "pang." Nor is it a distress signal. It is simply the alimentary tract accommodating itself to a reduced work load.

The best way to cope with sensations of hunger—those gnawing feelings in the stomach—is to drink water more frequently.

It is amazing how quickly and well a few sips of water can satisfy what feels like a ravenous appetite.

In the first week of the fast your tongue will become coated. The tongue is part of the elimination system. You may have bad breath, but remember, it is a healthy sign. Your tongue is a "mirror" that reflects the amount of waste matter being eliminated.

You may rinse your mouth with warm water, and you may brush your teeth and tongue very gently with a soft toothbrush. Do not use a mouthwash. No artificial colors, flavors or sweeteners should be used during a fast—mouthwashes contain all of these substances. Toothpastes contain artificial flavors and also should be avoided.

Natural disappearance of the tongue coating and of the acetone odor of the breath precede the return of appetite and are signs that the fast should be broken. The mouth then has a pleasant, fresh taste and the breath smells fresh.

23.

A Brief History of Fasting

Early Egyptians believed that the basis for preserving good health and youthfulness was a fast of three days a month. It apparently had beneficial results. The historian Herodotus described the Egyptians as an extremely healthy people.

The Protean figures in ancient Greece fasted. Pythagoras, the mathematician, was convinced that fasting aided the mental processes. He fasted 40 days at a time, and urged his students to do the same. Socrates and Plato enjoyed ten-day fasts. They claimed that fasting helped them to achieve the ultimate in cerebral functioning. Plutarch said: "Instead of using medicine, better fast today."

Spartans were raised to be spartan in their eating habits.

Aurelius Celsus fasted to treat his jaundice and epilepsy. The Arab physician Avicenna prescribed fasting for all ailments.

In ancient Japan a man could humiliate an enemy by camping on his doorstep and refusing to eat. Centuries ago in India prisoners resorted to fasting to soften their treatment by jailers. In both countries fasting is still commonplace, though the motivations have changed.

The ancient Hebrews fasted in mourning and in times of peril. They also fasted to express gratitude to God for His compassion in sparing them punishment, danger, or calamity. The Day of Atonement is still a day of fasting in the Hebrew calendar.

The Zends went without food every fifth day, the

Syrians every seventh, and the Mongolians every tenth.

Druid priests endured prolonged fasting before initiation into the mysteries of their cult.

Borrowing from the examples of Christ and the Apostles, the earliest Christians fasted on Wednesdays and Fridays—and, later, Saturdays.

Christians also turned to fasting in penance for any misfortune that befell them. In times of general disaster, a fast day was often proclaimed by a bishop.

The linking of almsgiving with fasting started through the custom of turning over to the poor those provisions saved on fast days.

It was once widely believed that demons entered the body of a man when he ate. To commune with God man first had to exorcise the demons and purify himself. He did this by abstaining from food. According to the Book of Matthew, "They goeth not out save by prayer and fasting."

In A.D. 110 Polycarp urged fasting as a way of warding off temptation and lust.

Fasting among Christians symbolized the suffering of Christ. Around the beginning of the fourth century, a time of great persecution, the Lenten fast was introduced. The 40-day abstention was meant to emulate the earlier examples of Moses, Jesus, and Elijah.

Arab physicians of the 10th and 11th centuries prescribed three-week fasts as a cure for syphilis and smallpox. During Napoleon's occupation of Egypt, hospitals used fasting as a treatment for venereal disease.

Ludwig Carnaro, a Venetian in the Renaissance, proposed fasting as the palliative for over-indulgence in the pleasures of food and drink. A year of strict dieting and occasional fasts restored his own health after it had been ravaged by years of dissipation. At the salty old age of 83 Carnaro wrote treatises that celebrated the benefits of fasting:

Poor, unfortunate Italy! Don't you see that gluttony leads to the death of your citizens, many more deaths than even a worldwide plague or a worldwide war? These disgraceful banquets which are now so popular have results equal to those of the most violent battles.

We must . . . eat only as much as is absolutely necessary for proper functioning of our body and use common sense. Any excess food gives us only the sensory pleasure of the moment but in the end we have to pay the consequences of sickness and sometimes even death.

In England a Dr. Chain (1671–1743) cured himself of the excesses of food and drink through fasting. He often prescribed his own "medicine": "I do not know how it is in other countries," Dr. Chain wrote, "but we Protestants do not consider . . . excess eating injurious. People look down on friends who are not able to stuff themselves at every meal. Doctors do not realize that they should be held responsible before society, their patients, and even the Creator for propagating excess eating and thus cutting short the lives of many of their patients."

Frederick Hoffman (1660–1742), a German, found fasting to be helpful in treating epilepsy, ulcers, plethora, cataracts, scurvy, and malignant ulcers. "In any illness," he declared, "it is best for the patient not to eat anything."

Russians came to a similar conclusion in the 18th and 19th centuries. In his *Report of Fasting as Prevention of Illness,* published in 1769, the University of Moscow's Professor Peter Veniaminov advised that it was best to stop eating completely during illness. "It gives the stomach a rest period, enabling the patient to digest properly when he recovers and starts to eat again."

B. G. Spassky, also of the University of Moscow, later reported success in treating intermittent fever with fasting. He said that it allows the growing processes in the body to take place without interference and "is thus a perfect remedy for chronic ailments."

Still another Russian, a 19th-century physician, Dr. Zealand by name, reported that fasting affected a patient's nervous system and his general health, digestion, and blood—all positively. "Fasting allows the body to rest and resume its normal activity with renewed strength," Dr. Zealand wrote.

Dating back to the Plymouth Colony, days of fasting were designated in colonial New England as ways of holding at bay a multitude of catastrophes: droughts, insect plagues, epidemic diseases, Indian wars, earthquakes and food shortages. Fast days were observed as scrupulously as the Puritan sabbath itself.

North American Indians held fasting in high esteem. Among the Algonquins the ability to forgo food for long periods of time was envied and admired as evidence of powers of endurance and fortitude. Hunters fasted before setting out for the kill.

Interest in fasting as a therapeutic tool began in this country during the last century. "Although beginning my practice in fog-covered medical superstition," Dr. Edward Dewey wrote a century ago, "I came to the conclusion that only nature can practice medicine." He prescribed fasting for stomach and intestinal disorders, obesity, dropsy, various infections and inflammations, elimination of physical weakness and flabbiness, and improvement of morale. It was his opinion that it is rest, not food, that repairs the nervous system and that eating causes as much tension as does work.

"I contend that during illness feeding becomes a burden to the sick," Dr. Dewey also wrote. "It uses energy that otherwise would be used to fight the illness."

The dramatic "hunger strike"—fasting in public—to protest political and social injustices is an age-old stratagem. It draws attention to a cause, and often results in remedial action. A fast carried on too long will cross the line into starvation, and few of the powers-that-be want to jeopardize their strength by creating martyrs.

A celebrated fast in Britain in the early 1900s was undertaken by a member of Mrs. Emmeline Pankhurst's Women's Social and Political Union. Marion Wallace Dunlop, a suffragette, fasted to protest a month's jail sentence for inscribing on the wall of the House of Commons a clause from the U.S. Bill of Rights. Hundreds of militant women—and some sympathetic males —joined Ms. Dunlop in the fast and were promptly jailed. In a typical British class action, they all then fasted in objection to their status as ordinary convicts.

Parliament passed a "cat and mouse" act, permitting hunger strikers judged to be in danger of collapse to leave prison for a few days. Once out, most of the fasters discreetly "got lost" and stayed lost. (Women got the vote in 1918.)

In modern times it was Gandhi who popularized fasting as a means of dramatizing a cause. Again it was British law that was successfully challenged.

A Sikh leader fasted for 47 days to persuade the government to establish a separate, Punjab-speaking state. A yogi and a swami fasted to gain assurance that the Punjab state would *not* be partitioned.

The renowned British biologist J. B. S. Haldane fasted for one week, when living in Calcutta, in protest of the U.S. Information Agency's "anti-scientific and anti-Indian activities."

Bridget Rose Dugdale, accused mastermind in the theft of $20-million worth of art treasures for Irish terrorists, fasted to force the transfer of four convicted terrorists from British to Irish jails.

In Russia the imprisoned Vladimir Bukovsky fasted when he was confined to solitary on charges of anti-Soviet agitation; he was joined in the fast by other prisoners. At Radcliffe College students fasted to protest housing rules.

24.

A Noble Tradition

Since the dawn of religion, fasting has been a ritual.

Demons were commonly thought to enter into the body of man through food. "He who wishes to have intercourse with God must thus be abstemious in order to become a pure vessel of the Spirit."

There are no less than 74 references to fasting in the Old and New Testaments. Here are just a few of them:

Moses fasted for 40 days and 40 nights before he received the Ten Commandments on Mount Sinai.

Elijah fasted for 40 days and 40 nights before reaching the Mount of God.

Daniel fasted before receiving divine revelation.

The Book of Chronicles declares that greater closeness with God was obtained throughout Judea by a declaration of a national fast.

Jesus fasted for 40 days and 40 nights.

"When you fast," the Book of Matthew states, "do not look dismal, like the hypocrites." And: "Be honest, be sincere. Fast for honest and truthful purposes."

The disciples of Eastern mysticism embrace fasting with fervor. Yogis fast in the hope of achieving new mystical revelations. In Japan the disciples of Buddha fast as an exercise in asceticism. Dr. Imamura Motoo, who has supervised many fasts, wrote: "Religious ascetics, who led their lives abstaining from food, came to the conclusion that fasting improved not only their spiritual state, but also their physical condition, and through fasting many diseases could be cured."

Edward J. Farrell, a writer specializing in books on

religion, has described fasting as a "religious value . . . having a marvelous resiliency and life span co-extensive with humanity itself. What the parents throw away as useless, the children bring back as new-found treasures. What one generation discards, the next generation unearths and enshrines . . . man should look to his inner resources, his unused power, his hidden self . . . [but] the consumer society generates its antithesis . . . fasting precedes the rebirth of nature, sowing and harvesting . . ."

Russian icon painters would fast at least one day before painting—to get ready, to get in the mood.

Pope Paul VI has said fasting would be a symbolic expression of solidarity with the world's poor. "Man must through fasting dispose himself even materially to allowing his neighbor to share his property in spite of the claims of self-love."

25.

Fasting, Feasting, and Fat

Henry VIII may have set a good table, but at the same time he set a bad example. To this day his name conjures up images of unrestrained gluttony.

The future King George IV, who was one of Henry's successors, also lived high off the hog. In 1817 he hosted a dinner party at Brighton Pavilion, with the famous chef Marie Antoine Carême presiding over this menu:

Consommé Madeira, with foie gras, truffles, mushrooms
River trout with tomato and garlic sauce
Poached turbot in lobster sauce
Eel festooned with cocks' combs
Braised goose
Salmon steak with herbs, butter, and anchovies
Sauteed pheasant segments with truffles
Breast of young wild rabbits
Stuffed partridges in aspic
Meadow larks en terrine with creamed chicken liver
  encased in oven-toasted bread

And these were only the appetizers!

Let George eat it. As delectable as such a Brobdingnagian feast must have been, it was hardly the kind of repast to promote good health and vigor.

Surely no one these days is eating like Henry or George. We are not eating as much as even our grandparents did, but—unlike our grandparents—we are overweight.

Most of us know the reason why we are overweight. We are taking in more fuel than we are burning up. We live in an automated, push-button culture that's made us soft, flabby, and lazy. But too many of us are eating as if we were gandy dancers, lumberjacks, or farmhands; we are also feeding on junk foods that supply us with a diet rich in "empty calories."

Anyone who is 30 pounds overweight is in effect carrying around a 30-pound bag everywhere he goes. Obesity is defined as being 20 percent over one's preferred weight—and more than 45-million Americans *fall* into this category, as we noted earlier.

Here are a few random observations on fat:

• In a study of obesity among adolescents, Dr. Jean Mayer found that fat girls were burning up far fewer calories than lean girls.

• Dr. Mayer also has reported: "In colleges where acceptance was conditioned on a personal interview, the obese girls had only one-third as good a chance of being accepted as their normal-weight classmates; the obese boys had half as good a chance."

• Dr. Walter Lyon Bloom observed that lean people average one hour a day less in bed and spend 23 percent more time on their feet than do the obese.

• Few fat people live out their biblical allotment of threescore and ten years. The only common cause of death that does not take the fat earlier than the lean is suicide.

• Being fat—as well as increasing the risk of heart attacks, high blood pressure, and diabetes—raises the possibility of having gallstones and gallbladder disorders, and makes one more prone to accidents.

• The fat may not know when they are hungry. People who are not overweight tend to eat only when they *are* hungry. ("If it is six o'clock, I am hungry and must have my dinner," the fat person reasons, even though it is only 4:00 P.M. and some trickster has set the hands of the clock ahead.)

• "Nobody loves a fat man, especially not himself," Dr. Theodore Rubin observed in Consumer Guide's *Rating the Diets*. "If he didn't need love so much, he probably would not be fat in the first place."

- "The fat," according to one well-publicized study, think of themselves as generally "unhappy, nervous, tense, and dissatisfied."
- Fat people are likely to try to eat their way out of trouble. As children, they may not have learned to tell the difference between hunger and fear. As adults, they do not know whether they are hungry or just distraught.
- Seating in public places is almost always an irksome problem for the fat, one often caused, noted "the unstylishly stout" Richard F. Shepard in *The New York Times,* by restrictive armrests or limited leg room.
- It is financially punitive to be fat. Obese people pay higher insurance premiums, and the cost for treating ailments induced by obesity can be prohibitive. A survey of 15,000 executives revealed that fat bosses receive less pay than lean bosses. Policemen and firemen have been ordered to trim down or face dismissal—shape up or ship out.
- The overweight are often undernourished. Poor diets, lacking in essential nutrients, are cheaper, and they are usually fat-making. (This explains why there are more poor fat people than rich fat people.)
- We may be born with genes that program us to be fat.
- Overfeeding an infant during the first six months of its life increases the fat in every body cell. This can lead to a life-long fate of being fat.
- Fat parents who want their fat children to lose weight would do well to get *themselves* in shape first. Setting an example is more persuasive than words—always.

26.

Fasting Away from Home

Since the mid-19th century, in clinics and sanitoriums in Switzerland, France, Russia, India, and Germany, fasting has been used in the treatment of patients suffering from metabolic disorders, allergic diseases, skin disorders, arthritis, asthma, ulcerative colitis, cardiovascular complaints, and grand mal epilepsy.

The fasting treatment has also had enthusiastic supporters in the United States—exclusive of the medical profession. (In spite of the overwhelming data—see pages 133–148 Bibliography—most of my colleagues are still not seriously interested in exploring its potentials.)

Lack of encouragement from the medical profession notwithstanding, fasting is entering the mainstream of American life. Thousands of us are making a place for it in our busy lives. With rising levels of health consciousness, more and more of us are choosing to take a vacation from eating when we take our vacation from work, a time that traditionally was devoted to promiscuous gorging.

A fasting vacation is best accomplished under supervision and in the company of others. There are a number of spas and retreats that offer fasting as part of a general health-building regimen. Their attractions usually include tranquil settings, sunshine, facilities for exercise, and carefully supervised diets of natural foods.

In the preparation of this book, we visited a few places where fasts are conducted, and we corresponded with others. The following are brief impressions of the facilities and programs but do not constitute endorsement.

Bay'n Gulf Hygienic Home. Set 900 feet back from the Gulf of Mexico, this "hygienic home" offers easy access to white sandy beaches and swimming. "The road to health" followed here begins with a fast and ends with a diet of natural foods. Sunshine, exercise, rest, relaxation, health discussions, and counseling make up the daily routine. The proclaimed goal is harmony between body and nature.

"Many people look 20 years younger after a 21-day fast," J. M. Brosious, the director of Bay'n Gulf, told us. "The only people who have not benefited from fasting here are those in terminal stages of Parkinson's disease, cancer, and multiple sclerosis. Arthritics have little or no pain after 14 days of fasting. By cleansing the brain of its toxic waste, the mind becomes clear again . . . vision improves . . . asthma, migraines, sciatica, and bursitis are ailments cured in a long fast . . ."

Television viewing is restricted to two hours a day. Vitamin supplements are discouraged; Mr. Brosious contends they "hamper the fasting state." He believes that a fast of at least ten days every six months is beneficial for everybody irrespective of the state of his health.

ADDRESS: Bay'n Gulf Hygienic Home, 18207–09 Gulf Boulevard, Redington Shores, St. Petersburg, Fla. 33708.

Esser's Hygienic Rest Ranch.   On 14 acres of Palm Beach County, this Florida ranch basks in almost perpetual sunshine, which is extolled here as "body-building therapy . . . in the promotion of health, vigor, and growth of cell structure." There are tennis and volleyball courts and facilities for hiking, biking, and weightlifting.

Many guests arrive at the ranch as invalids. The director, William L. Esser, says that "repair and regeneration of diseased or injured organs occur at a very rapid rate during fasting. Re-establishment of chemical imbalances also occurs. For example, in pernicious anemia an increase of red cells by 2- or 3-million during the course of a three-week fast is not unusual."

Every factor that is out of harmony ages us beyond our years, according to the tall, tanned, trim director, who—in his sprightly 60s—still vigorously plays tennis every day. The words of Paracelsus are revered at Esser's: "The physician who wants to know Man must look upon him as a whole, and not as a piece of patched-up work. If he finds a part of the human body diseased, he must look for the cause that produced the disease and not merely the external effects."

Mr. Esser's interest in the therapeutic powers of fasting dates back to his father's bout with tuberculosis. A fast in a sanitorium in Europe led to complete recovery.

After fasting at Esser's, guests are put on a diet largely drawn from fruits and vegetables organically grown at the ranch. Meat, fish, and poultry are not needed for health and vigor, in the opinion of the director.

Of the approximately 15,000 fasts Mr. Esser has supervised, he says he is probably the proudest of a "cure" involving a woman who was suffering from an apparently hopeless case of ileitis. She had consulted one specialist after another and had a long history of medication, but her condition steadily deteriorated. After a series of short fasts at Esser's, she made a complete recovery.

There are accommodations for about 30 guests.

ADDRESS: Esser's Hygienic Rest Ranch, P.O. Box 161, Lake Worth, Fla. 33460.

Pawling Health Manor. This retreat for all seasons is a complex of a large manor house, a motel-like annex, and a gymnasium set in the patrician Hudson River estate country 100 miles north of New York City. There is no programmed activity, and the guests are free to make day-excursions into the surrounding countryside, which is rich in historic associations.

Because of its location, the manor attracts a large number of New York-based actors, writers, and artists. The clientele here is almost exclusively made up of people who come to lose weight but are otherwise in good health.

The director, Robert Gross, has created an atmosphere that is permissive—up to a point. Guests may keep their own hours, come and go as they please, and look at television. But the least evidence of smoking is sufficient to get a guest expelled.

ADDRESS: Pawling Health Manor, P.O. Box 401, Hyde Park, N.Y. 12538.

Shelton's Health School. "Health is built—not bought" is the motto of the "school," which is pleasantly situated atop a secluded hill outside San Antonio. Herbert M. Shelton, the founder, has always contended that health cannot be gotten out of a bottle or pillbox or hypodermic syringe. "It is ours only as a consequence of obedience to the laws of life."

The *modus operandi* at Shelton's is extremely strict. There are the usual restrictions of tobacco, alcohol, stimulants, drugs, soft drinks, and "similar poisons." There is no television set on the premises. Listening to the radio is discouraged, as is reading newspapers. Lights must be out by 9:00 P.M. Emphasis is on rest —physical, mental, sensory, physiological.

One of Shelton's key theses is that "bodies learn to heal and to stay healed." Many of the desperately ill, who have been given up for hopeless by family and doctors alike, find their way here. No small proportion of them, the school claims, finds relief from an alphabet of ailments.

The Shelton Golden Rule: "If not comfortable in body and mind from one meal to the next, miss the next meal." Over 40,000 people have fasted here.

ADDRESS: Shelton's Health School, P.O. Box 1277, San Antonio, Tex. 78295.

Buchinger Clinics. There are two: one in West Germany, one in Spain. They were founded by Dr. Otto Buchinger, who supervised tens of thousands of fasts.

"By its deep-reaching results and its diversified possibilities of application," Dr. Buchinger observed, "the fasting therapy has far exceeded the expectations that I placed upon it. The whole system is brought under fasting's corrective influence. There is a metamorphosis in the total organism. The majority of acute and chronic ailments can be improved or alleviated by the long fast."

Dr. Buchinger's introduction to fasting came when he found it was successful in treating his own chronic arthritic rheumatism. He reached the same conclusion as Paracelsus: "He who fasts is in the hands of the inner physician."

Here, a minimum stay of three weeks is deemed necessary to get the full benefit of the "cure." Fasting is supplemented by homeopathic stimuli, thoracic compresses, enemas, colon irrigations, massages, gymnastic exercises, and bed rests. Doctors and nurses are in constant attendance. Initial medical exams are obligatory. A special effort is made to provide psychological equilibrium for new arrivals while they are in "this impressionable and receptive state."

After the fast, the guest is put on a transition refeeding schedule which progresses through a fruit diet to normal eating patterns. The leisurely consumption of the first formal "meal" assumes almost ritual significance at Buchinger. Two burning candles adorn the table and a handmade, decorated diploma at the plate documents the fast.

"Fasting is much easier than one generally imagines," the clinics reassure their guests. "You normally suffer no feeling of hunger or weakness. You can walk about, take part in games and sports and many other activities. It should be emphasized that for a proper and successful fasting cure it is vital to follow consistently our prescribed regulations (no alcohol, no cigarettes, and nothing eaten during the cure). You can thus breathe deeply and experience life at a new level of intensity."

ADDRESSES: Buchinger-Klinik am Bodensee, 777 Überlingen, Lake Constance, West Germany; Clinica Buchinger, Marbella, SA, Marbella (Malaga), Spain.

Villa Vegetariana. The villa, which is on the outskirts of Cuernavaca and about an hour's drive from Mexico City, has 36 guest units, a ceramic tile swimming pool, an outdoor gymnasium, hammocks and swings, and private solaria for nude sunbathing.

For more than 20 years the proprietor, David Stry,

has been a vegetarian and has fasted periodically. "Fasting," he says, "is economically sound. It is cosmetic. It gives the digestive system a complete rest. The body reverses itself. Fasting throws out toxins and waste matter that have accumulated in the body. Fasting is housecleaning."

A typical day at the villa is built around calisthenics, classes in eye exercises, yoga, group classes in conversational Spanish, sunbathing, bicycling, strolls through organic gardens, shopping and sightseeing, dancing on the poolside patio, and evening lectures or discussions.

After the fast, guests eat a herbivorous, frugivorous diet of fresh vegetables, seeds and nuts, and such indigenous fruits as mangoes, papayas, cherimoyas, tropical bananas, sapodillas, granadillas, melons, manzanas, annonas, guanabanas, chicos, berries, and avocados—most of which are grown on the premises.

Mr. Stry likes to remind vegetarians that they are in good company: Buddha, Plato, Socrates, Plutarch, Diogenes, Milton, Pope, Tolstoy, Shelley, Newton, Voltaire, Rousseau, Edison, Shaw, Schweitzer, and Hans Holzer.

Management prefers that anyone planning to fast here should have previous fasting experience or be knowledgeable about fasting.

ADDRESS: Villa Vegetariana, P.O. Box 1228, Cuernavaca, Mexico.

The Cormillot Clinic. Almost everybody who comes to this clinic in the heart of Buenos Aires has an obesity problem. The clientele is international, and 90 percent of it is female. Many arrive here in desperation after they have failed at every "sensible" reducing diet.

Dr. Alberto Cormillot, who is psychoanalytically trained, is convinced that the causes of obesity are rooted in psychological disturbances. He makes available at the clinic supportive therapy on either an individual or a group basis.

Patients are encouraged to exercise. They are free to leave the clinic and take advantage of the city's many cultural facilities.

During the autumn of 1974 I consulted with Dr.

Cormillot at his clinic and he later visited me in New York City. I should like to report a few of his observations:

• The obese men and women who profit the most from fasting are those who are 50 percent over-weight —and have been over-weight only as adults—and have some degree of emotional stability. Less progress is made by those people who are dependent on drugs of any kind—amphetamines, sleeping pills, alcohol, diuretics, and the like.

• Once the patient discovers that he can stop eating, he finds new possibilities within himself.

• While fasting, many of the women express more interest in having sexual intercourse, and they say they get more satisfaction from it.

• Phobias and inhibitions lessen their grip.

• Digestive disorders disappear almost completely after the first week.

• Menstruation becomes regular.

• Breathing, metabolism, and ovarian problems are improved, and the burden on the heart is alleviated.

• Fasting is better tolerated than a one-food diet.

• The appearance of the skin quickly improves. Blemishes disappear.

ADDRESS: The Cormillot Clinic, Paraguay 3358, Buenos Aires, Argentina.

Bibliography

Adler, Nathan. "Paris Had Its Hippies in the 1830s: They Drove the Establishment Mad," *Perspectives on Drugs and Drug Use,* no. 3 (1970): 55–59.

Altman, Lawrence K. "Soft Water Tied to Heart Attacks," *New York Times,* June 3, 1974.

America. "To Fast or Not to Fast," March 31, 1962: 849.

American Heart Association. "Diet and Coronary Heart Disease" (1973).

Andersen, Mogens. "Fasting Electrocardiogram," *ACTA Medica Scandinavica,* 187 (1970).

———. Letter to Jerome Agel, June 25, 1974.

Aoki, Thomas T., et al. "Hormonal Regulation of Glutamine Metabolism in Fasting Man," *Advances in Enzyme Regulation* 10 (1972):145–51.

Azar, Gordon and Bloom, Walter. "Ketones, Nonesterified Fatty Acids, and Nitrogen Excretion," *Archives of Internal Medicine* 112, no. 3 (1963):343.

Babayanz, R. "'Natural Stimulator,'" *Nediela (Izvestia),* April 5, 1970.

Babayanz, R., et al. "The Experience of Using Fasting-Diet Therapy in Dermatology," *Vestnik Dermatalogic i Venerologic* 7, no. 8 (1972).

Baird, I. MacLean. Letter to Jerome Agel, June 10, 1974.

Baird, I. MacLean and Howard, Alan N. "Obesity: Medical and Scientific Aspects," *Proceedings of the First Symposium of The Obesity Association of Great Britain,* London (1968).

Ball, Michael F. "Tissue Change During Intermittent Starvation and Caloric Restriction as Treatment for Severe Obesity," *Archives of Internal Medicine* 125 (1970):62–68.

Ballantyne, D. A. Letter to Editor, *British Medical Journal,* Aug. 7, 1971: 370.

———. Letter to Jerome Agel, June 15, 1974.

Barkas, Janet. *The Vegetable Passion: A History of the Vege-*

tarian State of Mind (New York: Scribner's, 1975).

Baruh, Selum, et al. "Fasting Hypoglycemia," *Medical Clinics of North America* 57, no. 6 (1973).

Benedict, Ruth Fulton. "The Vision in Plains Culture," *American Anthropologist* 24 (1922):1–22.

Better Homes & Gardens. "Fasting," Feb. 1961.

Bieler, Henry G. *Food Is Your Best Medicine* (New York: Random House, 1965).

Bishop, Jerry E. "Cancer vs. What You Eat," *Science Digest*, March 1974: 10–14.

Bloom, Walter. "Fasting as an Introduction to the Treatment of Obesity," *Metabolism* 8 (1959):214–20.

———. "Fasting Ketosis in Obese Men and Women," *Journal of Laboratory and Clinical Medicine* 59 (1962):605–12.

———. "Inhibition of Salt Excretion by Carbohydrate," *Archives of Internal Medicine* 109, no. 1 (1962).

———. "Obesity and Energy Expenditure," *Journal of the Medical Association of Georgia* 56, no. 9 (1967):381–82.

Bloom, Walter and Azar, Gordon. "Changes in Heart Size and Plasma Volume During Fasting," *Metabolism* 15, no. 5 (1966):409–13.

———. "Similarities of Carbohydrate Deficiency and Fasting," *Archives of Internal Medicine* 112, no. 3 (1963):333–43.

Bloom, Walter and Mitchell, William. "Salt Excretion of Fasting Patients," *Archives of Internal Medicine* 106, no. 3 (1960): 321–25.

Bonnet, F., et al. "Free Fatty Acid Pattern in the Plasma of Normal and Obese Children During Fasting and Intravenous Glucose Tolerance Test," *Archives of Int. Physiol. BioChim.* 78, no. 3 (1970): 495–508.

Boulter, Philip R., et al. "Dissociation of the Renin-Aldosterone System and Refractorines to the Sodium-Retaining Action of Mineralocorticoid During Starvation in Man," *Journal of Clinical Endocrinology and Metabolism* 38, no. 2 (1974): 248–54.

Bragg, Paul C. *The Miracle of Fasting* (Santa Ana, Calif.: Health Science, 1973).

Braly, Malcolm. "Terror Stalks the Fat Farm," *Playboy*, Jan. 1974.

Brodsky, Greg. *From Eden to Aquarias: The Book of Natural Healing* (New York: Bantam Books, 1974).

Brosius, J. M. Report to Jerome Agel, 1974.

Brožek, Josef. "Psychology of Human Starvation and Nutritional Rehabilitation," *Scientific Monthly* 70 (1950):270–74.

Bruce, David L. "Anesthetic Implications of Fasting," *Anesth. Analg.* 50, no. 4 (1971):612-19.

Bruch, Hilde. *Eating Disorders* (New York: Basic Books, 1973).

Brown, David F., et al. "Fasting and Postprandial Serum Triglyceride Levels in Healthy Young Americans," *American Journal of Clinical Nutrition* 13, no. 1 (1963):1–7.

Buchinger, Otto H. F. *Everything You Want to Know About Fasting* (New York: Pyramid Books, 1972).

———. "Über Moderne Heilfasten Juren" ("About Modern Fasting Cures"), Buchinger Clinics (1970).

———. "What 40,000 Fasting Treatments Have Taught Me," Buchinger Clinics.

Buchwald, Art. "The Secret of Dieting," *Food and Fitness*.

Butz, Earl L. Statement by the Secretary of Agriculture Before the Subcommittee on Agricultural Production, Marketing and Stabilization of Prices, U.S. Senate, March 21, 1974.

Cahill, George F., Jr. "How Fasting Works," *New England Journal of Medicine* 282 (1970):668–75.

———. "Physiology of Insulin in Man," *Diabetes* 20, no. 12 (1971):785–99.

Cahill, George F., Jr., et al. "The Consumption of Fuels During Prolonged Starvation," *Advances in Enzyme Regulation* 6 (1967):143–50.

———. "Fat and Nitrogen Metabolism in Fasting Man," *Hormone and Metabolic Research*, Supp. 2 (1970).

———. "Hormone Fuel Interrelationships During Fasting," *Journal of Clinical Investigation* 45, no. 11 (1966):1751–67.

Carlson, A. J. and Hoelzel, F. "The Alleged Disappearance of Hunger During Starvation," *Science* 115 (1952):526–27.

Carlson, Anton J., et al. *Machinery of the Body* (Chicago: University of Chicago Press, 1961).

Cavagnini, F., et al. Letter to Editor, *British Medical Journal*, May 19, 1971: 527.

Chase, Alice. *Nutrition for Health* (West Nyack, N.Y.: Parker Publishing Co., 1970).

Chaussain, J. L. "Glycemic Response to 24 Hour Fast in Normal Children and Children with Ketotic Hypoglycemia," *Journal of Pediatrics* 82, no. 3 (1973):438–43.

Christensen, Niels Juel. "Plasma Norepinephrine and Epinephrine in Untreated Diabetics, During Fasting and After Insulin Administration," *Diabetes* 23, no. 1 (1974).

Christianity Today. "Fasting as Therapy," May 12, 1972: 12.

Claiborne, Craig. "The Cure in Italy: Strict Diet, Plus That Funny Tasting Water," *New York Times*, July 11, 1974.

Clark, Blake. "A Swift, Sure Way to Take Off Weight," *Reader's Digest*, Nov. 1962: 115–18.

Cloud, Wallace. "After the Green Revolution," *Sciences*, Oct. 1973.

Corseri, Gary. "Fast, Fast, Fast!", *The New York Times*, March 12, 1975, Op-Ed page.

Costamaillere, L., et al. "Experience With Diagnosis and Treatment of Fasting Hypoglycemia," *Revista Medica de Chile* 100, no. 6 (1972):656–64.

Cott, Allan. "Controlled Fasting Treatment of Schizophrenia in U.S.S.R.," *Schizophrenia* 3, no. 1 (1971):2–10.

Craddock, Denis. *Obesity and Its Management* (Edinburgh: E. & S. Livingstone, 1969).

Crahay, Roland. "Psychology of Fasting," *Abbottempo* (Chicago: Abbott Laboratories).

Cravario, A., et al. *Report on Fasting of 25 Obese Females.*

Cravetto, C. A. "Metabolic Aspects After Prolonged Fasting in Obese Subjects," *Folia Endocrinologica* 26, no. 2 (1973): 139–52.

Critchfield, Richard. "The Sputtering 'Green Revolution,'" *Nation,* Sept. 10, 1973: 207–11.

Cromey, Robert. "For God's Sake, Fast For Your Own Sake!" *Christian Century,* Feb. 28, 1968: 254.

Cubberly, Peter T., et al. "Lactic Acidosis and Death After The Treatment of Obesity by Fasting," *New England Journal of Medicine* 272, no. 12 (1965):628–30.

Current Literature. "'The Fasting Cure' Found Wanting by a Gastronomic Authority," 51 (1911):163–65.

———. "Table Talk: Concerning Eating and Drinking," 35 (1903):761.

Current Therapy. "Obesity: Method of Walter Lyon Bloom" (1960).

DeVries, Arnold. *Therapeutic Fasting* (Los Angeles: Chandler Book Co., 1963).

Drenick, Ernst J. "Weight Reduction by Prolonged Fasting," *Medical Times* 100, no. 1 (1972):209–30.

Drenick, Ernst J. and Dennin, H. F. "Energy Expenditure in Fasting Obese Men," *Journal of Laboratory and Clinical Medicine* 81, no. 3 (1973):421–30.

Drenick, Ernst J., et al. "Body Potassium Content in Obese Subjects and Potassium Depletion During Prolonged Fasting," *American Journal of Clinical Nutrition* 18, no. 4 (1966): 278–85.

———. "Effect on Hepatic Morphology of Treatment of Obesity by Fasting, Reducing Diets and Small-Bowel Bypass," *New England Journal of Medicine* 282, no. 15 (1970): 829–34.

———. "Magnesium Depletion During Prolonged Fasting of Obese Males," *Journal of Clinical Endocrinology and Metabolism* 29, no. 10 (1969):1341–48.

———. "Prolonged Starvation as Treatment for Severe Obesity," *Journal of the American Medical Association* 187, no. 2 (1964):140–45.

Duncan, Garfield G. "Obesity—Some Consideration of Treatment," *American Journal of Clinical Nutrition* 13 (1963): 199.

Duncan, Garfield G. "Contraindications and Therapeutic Results of Fasting in Obese Patients," *Annals of New York Academy of Sciences* 131, Art. 1 (1965):632–36.

———. "The Control of Obesity by Intermittent Fasts," *Medical Clinics of North America* 48, no. 5 (1964):1359–72.

———. "Correction and Control of Intractable Obesity," *Journal of the American Medical Association* 181, no. 4 (1962):99–102.

———. "Intermittent Fasts in the Correction and Control of Intractable Obesity," *American Journal of the Medical Sciences* 245, no. 5 (1963):515–19.

Duncan, L. J. P., et al. "Phenmetrazine Hydrochloride and Methyl Cellulose in the Treatment of 'Refractory' Obesity," *Lancet* i (1960):1262–65.

Ebony. "Hints on Keeping Slim from Famous Personalities," November 1974.

Edison, Thomas A. "Edison on How to Live Long," *Hearst's Magazine,* 23 (1913): 266–69.

Ehret, Arnold. *Rational Fasting: A Scientific Method of Fasting Your Way to Health* (New York: Benedict Lust Publications, 1971).

Encyclopaedia Britannica, 1973 ed., "Fasting."

Encyclopedia Judaica, 1971 ed., "Fasting and Fast Days," 6:1190–96.

Ende, Norman. "Starvation Studies With Special Reference to Cholesterol," *American Journal of Clinical Nutrition* 11, no. 4 (1962):270–80.

Farrell, Edward J. "The Fast of the Body and the Hunger of the Spirit," *New Catholic World,* March/April 1974: 64–68.

Fernstrom, John D., and Wurtman, Richard J. "Nutrition and the Brain," *Scientific American,* 230, no. 2 (1974): pp. 84–91.

Fioravanti, Robert V. "Seeks Personal Stories on Hypoglycemia," Letter to Editor, *Prevention,* Oct. 1973.

Forbes, Gilbert B. "Weight Loss During Fasting: Implications for the Obese," *American Journal of Clinical Nutrition* 23, no. 9 (1970):1212–19.

Fosburgh, Lacey. "Scientist Fears Wide Food Shortage," *New York Times,* Feb. 28, 1974.

Fox, George. "Wanted: A Science of Nutrition," *Prevention,* May 1974: 59–64.

Fox, J. DeWitt. "Fasting for Fitness," *Life & Health* 80, no. 1 (1965):6–7.

Franklin, Maxine A. and Skoryna, Stanley C. "Studies in Natural Gastric Flora: Survival of Bacteria in Fasting Human Subjects," *Canadian Medical Association Journal* 105 (1971):380–86.

Fredericks, Carlton. "Hotline to Health," *Prevention,* July 1973: 59.

Fredholm, Bertil B. "Effects of Fasting on Adipose Tissue in situ in Young Dogs," *Scandinavian Journal of Clinical and Laboratory Investigation* 31, no. 1 (1973):79–86.

Galloway, John A. "The Effects of Low Doses of Intravenous Proinsulin and Insulin Combination in Normal Fasted Man," *Journal of Laboratory and Clinical Medicine* 78, no. 6 (1972):991–92.

Gamble, J. L., et al. "The Metabolism of Fixed Base During Fasting," *Journal of Biological Chemistry* 57 (1923):633–95.

Gandhi, M. K. *Gandhi's Autobiography* (1954 ed.).

———. "Why I Fasted for Twenty-one Days," *World Tomorrow* 16 (1933):496–97.

Garnett, E. S., et al. "Gross Fragmentation of Cardiac Myofibrils After Therapeutic Starvation for Obesity," *Lancet* i (1969).

Gasner, Douglas Brian. "The Perils of Lead," *World*, Aug. 1, 1972: 52.

Gault, John. "Prolonged Fasting Tested as Schizophrenia Therapy," *Medical Post*, Nov. 16, 1971: 16.

Genuth, Saul M. "Alanine Administration During Prolonged Fasting," *Medical Post*, Nov. 16, 1971.

Gibinski, Kornel. "Starvation Treatment of Obesity," *Polska Tygodnik Lekarski* 24, no. 25 (1969):951–64.

Gilliland, I. C. "Total Fasting in the Treatment of Obesity," *Postgraduate Medical Journal* 44 (1968):507.

Gligore, V. and Fekete, T. "Complete Fasting Diet (0-Calorie diet) in the Treatment of Obesity," *Revue Roumaine d'Endocrinologie* 10, no. 1 (1973):79–84.

Glueck, Grace H. "Fine Art of Fasting," *New York Times Magazine*, Oct. 8, 1961: 106.

Gol, Barbara. "Fasting: A Radical Medical Approach to Weight Loss," *Town & Country*, Jan. 1973: 32.

Goldman, Ronald, et al., "Yom Kippur, Air France, Dormitory Food, and the Eating Behavior of Obese and Normal Persons," *Journal of Personality and Social Psychology* 10, no. 2 (1968):117–23.

Greene, Gael. Letter to Jerome Agel, Dec. 1974.

Gross, Robert R. "In Defense of Fasting: A Rebuttal to Critiques in Playboy Magazine," *Natural Hygienews*, May 1974.

Grosser, Volker, et al. "Tryptophan Loading During Fasting," *Deutsche Gesundheitwesen*, April 4, 1973: 793–98.

Halloran, Richard. "Japanese Long in Jungle in Fine Health," *New York Times*, April 24, 1974.

Halsell, Grace. "Wisdom on the Hoof," *The New York Times*, March 1, 1975.

Harrison, Michael T. "The Long-Term Value of Fasting in the Treatment of Obesity," *Lancet* ii (1966).

Hauck, Charles R. "How to Break the Nutrition Habit," *New York Times,* Feb. 11, 1974.

Havemann, Ernest. "The Wasteful, Phony, Crash Dieting Craze," *Life,* Jan. 19, 1959: 102–106.

Henderson, J. S. "The Modulation in Fasted Hosts of a Tumor's Growth and the Contrasting Stability of Its Intrinsic Grade of Malignancy," *Journal of Pathology* 109, no. 1 (1973).

Hendrikx, A. and De Moor, P. "Metabolic Changes in Obese Patients During Fasting and Refeeding," *ACTA Clinica Belgica* 24, no. 1 (1969):1–16.

Hermann, L. S. and Iversen, M. "Death During Starvation," Letter to the Editor, *Lancet* ii (1968):217.

Hermann, L. S., et al. "Hyperaldosteronism Following Weight Reduction by Complete Fasting" and "Late Results of Weight Reduction by Complete Fasting," *Videnskab Og Praksis,* Jan. 30, 1969.

Hess, John L. "The Unbalanced American's Diet: 20 Partials, Not 'Three Squares'," *The New York Times,* Jan. 3, 1974.

Heyden, Siegfried H. "Now—The Workingman's Diet," *Reader's Digest,* Jan. 1972.

Heyden, Siegfried H., et al. "Body Weight and Cigarette Smoking As Risk Factors," *Archives of Internal Medicine* 128 (1971):915–19.

———. "Diet Treatment of Obese Hypertensives," *Clinical Science and Molecular Medicine* 45 (1973):209s–12s.

———. "Weight and Weight History in Relation to Cerebrovascular and Ischemic Heart Disease," *Archives of Internal Medicine* 128 (1971):956–60.

———. "Weight Reduction in Adolescents," *Nutrition and Metabolism* 15 (1973):295–304.

Hippocrates Health Institute. Letter to Jerome Agel, July 2, 1974.

Hittleman, Richard L. *Weight Control Through Yoga* (New York: Bantam Books, 1971).

Howard, A. N. Letters to Jerome Agel, April 8 and June 4, 1974.

Howard, Jane. "How I Lost 14 Pounds in a Week," *Family Circle,* Oct. 1974.

Hunscher, Martha A. "A Posthospitalization Study of Patients Treated for Obesity by a Total Fast Regimen," *Metabolism* 15, no. 5 (1966):383–93.

Imaichi, Kunitaro, et al. "Plasma Lipid Fatty Acid During Fasting," *American Journal of Clinical Nutrition* 13, no. 4 (1963):226–31.

Independent. "The Fast Cure—For Fasting," 84 (1915):436.

———. "Fasting as a Religious Experience," Editorial, 56 (1904):980–82.

Innes, J. A., et al. "Long-Term Follow-Up of Therapeutic Starvation," *British Medical Journal* 2 (1974):356–59.

Jahn, Mike. "Fasting Is So Spiritual," *Cosmopolitan,* July 1974.

Johnson, Thomas A. "Monsoon Shift Held Threat to World Food Supply," *New York Times,* Jan. 26, 1974.

Journal of the American Medical Association. "Starvation and Obesity" (Editorial), 187, no. 2 (1964):144.

————. "Three Views of the Treatment and Hazards of Obesity," 186, no. 7 (1963):45–50.

Kahan, Alexander. Letter to the Editor, *Lancet* i (1968):1378.

Kalkhoff, R. K. and Kim, H. J. "Metabolic Responses to Fasting and Ethanol Infusion in Obese, Diabetic Subjects," *Diabetes* 22, no. 5 (1973):372–80.

Katz, Sidney. "Metro Man Recovers from Mental Illness by Fasting 28 Days," *Toronto Star,* Aug. 26, 1972.

Klein, Frederick C. "New Techniques Help Pupils Who Can't Grasp Fundamental Concepts," *Wall Street Journal,* Nov. 17, 1970.

Klemesrud, Judy. "A Week at a Health Manor on the Last Resort Diet: Fasting," *New York Times,* Oct. 29, 1974.

Knobe, Bertha Damaris. "Why I Fasted Fifteen Days," *Ladies Home Journal* 29 (1912).

Knudsen, Kermit B. "Porphyria Precipitated by Fasting," *New England Journal of Medicine* 277, no. 7 (1967).

Knutsson, Karl Eric. "Fasting in Ethiopia. An Anthropological and Nutritional Study," *American Journal of Clinical Nutrition* 23, no. 7 (1970):956–69.

Kollar, Edward J. and Atkinson, Roland M. "The Effectiveness of Fasting in the Treatment of Superobesity," *Psychosomatics* 10, no. 2 (1969).

Komarnicka, R. "Treatment of Obesity with Starvation and Low Calorie Diet," *Polska Tygodnik Lekarski* 29, no. 20 (1974):843–45.

Lageder, H., et al. "Absolute Fasting as Therapy in Patients With Diabetes and Hyperlipaemia," *Wiener Klinische Wochenschrift,* March 23, 1973, p. 186.

Laszlo, J. "Changes in the Obese Patient and His Adipose Tissue During Prolonged Starvation," *Southern Medical Journal* 58 (1965):1099–1108.

Lawlor, T. Letter to Editor. *Lancet* i (1969).

Lawlor, T. and Wells, D. G. "Fasting as a Treatment of Obesity," *Postgraduate Medical Journal,* June Suppl., 1971: 452–58.

————. "Metabolic Hazards of Fasting," *American Journal of Clinical Nutrition* 22, no. 8 (1969):1142–49.

Lennox, William G. "A Study of the Retention of Uric Acid During Fasting," *Journal of Biological Chemistry* 66, no. 2 (1925): 521–72.

Lewis, Anthony. "Affluence and Survival II," *New York Times*, April 22, 1974.

Lissner, Will. "Cooke Asks a Fast to Back Africans," *New York Times*, July 6, 1974.

Literary Digest. "The Dangers of Fasting," 101 (1929): 23.

———. "Facts About Fasting," 95 (1927): 26.

———. "Holy Hunger: Tennessee Mountaineer Believes Fasting Was Divine Command," 123 (1937).

———. "Man a Poor Faster," 114 (1932): 18.

———. "The Starvation Cure," 76 (1923): 77.

Living Age. "The Spirit of Fasting," (1910).

Maagoe, H. and Mogensen, E. F. "The Effect of Treatment on Obesity: A Follow-up Investigation of a Material Treated with Complete Starvation," *Danish Medical Bulletin* 17, no. 7 (1970): 206–9.

Macadam, Robert F. and Jackson, A. M. Letter to the Editor, *Lancet* i, May 24, 1969.

McCarthy, Colman. "Fasting: Just Another Fad, or Nation's 'Finest Hour,' " *Washington Post Service*, Dec. 28, 1974.

McCoy, Kathy. "Winning the Weight War," *Teen*, May 1974: 39.

MacCuish, A. C., et al. "Follow-up Study of Refractory Obesity Treated by Fasting," *British Medical Journal* 1, (1968): 91–92.

McGraw, James R. and Fulton, Alvenia M., eds. *Dick Gregory's Natural Diet for Folks Who Eat: Cooking with Mother Nature* (New York: Harper & Row, 1973).

McHarry, Charles. "On the Town," *New York News*, June 8, 1974.

McMillan, Thelma J. "Your Basic Food Needs: Nutrients For Life, Growth," *Yearbook of Agriculture* (1969): 254–59.

Mahler, H. "Better Food for a Healthier World," *World Health*, Feb/March 1974: 3.

Marliss, Errol B., et al. "Glucagon Levels and Metabolic Effects in Fasting Man," *Journal of Clinical Investigation* 49, no. 12 (1970): 2256–70.

Mayer, Jean. *Human Nutrition* (Springfield, Ill.: C. C. Thomas, 1972), chap. 36, "Reducing by Total Fasting."

———. "Obese Are Fair Game for Discrimination," *New York News*, Feb. 26, 1975.

———. *Overweight: Causes, Cost, and Control* (Englewood Cliffs, N. J.: Prentice-Hall, 1968: 161–62.

Medical World News. "In Three Months, Even Autistic Children Respond," Sept. 24, 1971.

Middlebury, Maria. "My Week Without Food," *Good Housekeeping* 53 (1911): 202.

Miller, Arthur. "Sakharov, Détente and Liberty," *New York Times*, July 5, 1974.

Morgulis, Sergius. "Fasting and the Healing Art," *Hygeia* 8 (1930):609–13.

Mottram, R. F. and Baker, Patricia G. B. "Metabolism of Exercising and Resting Human Skeletal Muscle in the Post Prandial and Fasting States," *Clinical Science* 44 (1973): 479–91.

Munro, J. F. and Duncan, L. J. P. "Fasting in the Treatment of Obesity," *Practitioner* 208 (1972): 493–98.

Munro, J. F., et al. "Further Experience With Prolonged Therapeutic Starvation in Gross Refractory Obesity," *British Medical Journal* 4 (1970): 712–14.

NBC News. "You're Too Fat," 1974.

New Catholic Encyclopedia, 1967 ed., 5:847–50.

New Schaff-Herzog Encyclopedia of Religious Knowledge, 1967 ed.: 279–84.

New York News. "Fat Bosses Pull In Their Moneybelts," Jan. 2, 1974: 16.

———. "Jaw Lock Ends Lip Service to Diet," Dec. 1, 1973.

———. "The Thin Girl Within the 'Fat' Person Comes Out," April 18, 1974: 91.

New York Post. "Dieting With Taft's Choice," March 5, 1975.

———. "Fasting for a World of Plenty," Nov. 21, 1974: 17.

The New York Times. "Harry Wills Dead," Dec. 22, 1958: 2.

———. "Sakharov Ends 6-Day Fast," July 5, 1974.

———. "Soviet Prisoners Reported Joining Bukovsky in Fast," April 15, 1972.

New Yorker. "Books: From Abalone to Zimmern, Sir Alfred," Nov. 12, 1973.

Newsweek. "Fast, Fast, Fast," April 15, 1963.

———. "Pangs of Conscience, January 20, 1975: 72.

———. "Running Out of Food?" April 1, 1974: 40–41.

———. "Strictly from Hunger," Nov. 22, 1971: 122–24.

Nikolayev, Yuri. Letter to Dr. Allan Cott, May 1974.

Null, Gary and staff. *The Complete Question and Answer Book of General Nutrition* (New York: Dell, 1974).

Nutrition Reviews. "Changes in Liver Histology and Function in Fasted Human Subjects," 25, no. 10 (1967):295–97.

———. "Hunger During Total Starvation Regimen," 25, no. 2 (1967):40–41.

———. "Lipid Accumulation in Heart Muscle During Fasting," 23, no. 1 (1965):14–16.

———. "Long-Term Changes in Body Weight Following Complete Fasting for Obesity," 25, no. 6 (1967):168–70.

———. Potassium Supplementation During Fasting for Obesity," 28, no. 7 (1970):177–78.

———. "Salt Supplementation During Fasting in the Cold," 23, no. 2 (1965):45–46.

Oldfield, Josiah. *Fasting for Health and Life* (London, 1924).

Olefsky, Jerrold, et al. "Effects of Weight Reduction on Obesity," *Journal of Clinical Investigation* 53, no. 1 (1974): 64–76.

Owen, Philip and Cahill, George F., Jr., "Metabolic Effects of Exogenous Glucocorticoids in Fasted Man," *Journal of Clinical Investigation* 52 (1973):2596–604.

Owen, Philip, et al. "Brain Metabolism During Fasting," *Journal of Clinical Investigation* 46, no. 10 (1967).

———. "Liver and Kidney Metabolism During Prolonged Starvation," *Journal of Clinical Investigation* 48 (1969):574.

Pager, Milton and Iampietro, P. F. "The Effect of Prolonged Cold and Starvation and Subsequent Refeeding on Plasma Lipids and Glucose of Normal Men," *Metabolism: Clinical and Experimental* 15, no. 1 (1966):9–16.

Parekh, Manilal C. "Fasting as a Cure for Lynching," *Christian Century,* 52 (1935).

Parker, Donal, et al. "Persistence of Rhythmic Human Growth Hormone Release During Sleep in Fasted and Nonisocalorically Fed Normal Subjects," *Metabolism: Clinical and Experimental* 21, no. 3 (1972):241.

Parnell, R. W. "Fragmentation of Cardiac Myofibrils After Therapeutic Starvation," *Lancet* i (1969):1154.

———. Letter to the Editor, *Lancet* i (1969).

Parrett, O. S. "Fasting," *Life & Health,* April 1965: 24–26.

Patient Care. A Special Issue. "A Practical Approach to Diet Compliance," April 1, 1973.

Peters, G. "Fasting Cures," *Medizinische Klinik* 63, no. 31 (1968):1209–11.

Porter, A. M. W. Letter to the Editor, *Lancet* i (1968): 1378.

Porter, Sylvia. "Staple Inflation," *New York Post,* May 28, 1974.

Prevention. "Fasting Can Control Schizophrenia," Aug. 1971: 197–201.

Punch. Jan. 9, 1974: 46.

Randolph, Theron G. "Food Addiction and Ecologic Mental Illness" (Chicago: Human Ecology Research Foundation, 1971).

———. "Food Addiction, Obesity and Alcoholism," *International Journal of Social Psychiatry,* Congress issue (1964).

———. Letter to Jerome Agel, June 14, 1974.

———. "The Realities of Food Addiction: 1. Description and Recognition; 2. Treatment and Prophylaxis," *Health Views & News,* nos. 10–11 (1971).

Rath, Rathmer and Masek, Josef. "Changes in the Nitrogen Metabolism in Obese Women after Fasting and Refeeding," *Metabolism: Clinical & Experimental* 15, no. 1 (1966):1–8.

Read, Piers Paul. *Alive* (Philadelphia: Lippincott, 1974).

Reed, Roy. "U.S. Fertilizer Shortage Expected to Be Damaging to Many Poorer Nations," *New York Times,* April 4, 1974.

Robbins, William. "U.S. Needy Found Poorer, Hungrier Than 4 Years Ago," *New York Times,* June 20, 1974, p. 1.

Rochlin, Isidore and Edwards, W. L. Jack. "The Misinterpretation of Electrocardiograms with Postprandial T-wave Inversion," *Circulation* 10 (1954):843–49.

Rooth, G. Letters to Jerome Agel, April 30 and June 18, 1974.

Rooth, G. and Carlström, S. "Therapeutic Fasting," *ACTA Medica Scandinavica* 187 (1970):455–63.

Rooth, G. and Ostenson, S. "Acetone Alveolar Air and the Control of Diabetes," *Lancet* ii (1966).

Rooth, G., et al. "Plasma Tocopherol Levels in Therapeutic Starvation," *International Journal of Vitamin & Nutrition Research* 41 (1971):355–59.

Rothenberg, Robert B. *The Fast Diet Book* (New York: Grosset & Dunlap, 1971).

Runcie, J. "Urinary Sodium and Potassium Excretion in Fasting Obese Subjects," *British Medical Journal* 2 (1971):22–25.

Runcie, J. and Hilditch, T. E. "Energy Provision, Tissue Utilization and Weight Loss in Prolonged Starvation," *British Medical Journal,* May 18, 1974: 352–56.

Runcie, J. and Thomson, T. J. "Prolonged Starvation—A Dangerous Procedure?" *British Medical Journal* 3 (1970): 432–35.

———. "Total Fasting, Hyperuricaemia and Gout," *Postgraduate Medical Journal* 45 (1969):251–53.

Schachter, Stanley. "Obesity and Eating," *Science* 161 (1968): 751–56.

Schanche, Don A. "Diet Books That Poison Your Mind and Harm Your Body," *Today's Health* 52, no. 4 (1974): 56–61.

Schloeder, Francis X., and Steinbaugh, Bobby J. "Defect of Urinary Acidification During Fasting," *Metabolism* 15, no. 1 (1966):17–25.

Schmeck, Harold J., Jr. "Alcoholism Cost to Nation Put at $25-Billion a Year," *New York Times,* July 11, 1974: 1.

———. "World Seen Near a Food Disaster," *New York Times,* March 15, 1974.

Schrub, J.-Cl., et al. "Lipid Changes Induced by Fasting in Obese Subjects," *Semaine des Hopitaux* 49, 19 (1973):1349–56.

Science Digest. "Fasting Record," April 1967: 57.

———. "New 'S' Diet," Feb. 1974: 54.

———. "New Slimming Device," Feb. 1974.

Science News. "Famine and the Third World," 105 (May 11, 1974).

———. "High Protein Diet and Cholesterol," 105 (1974):240.

———. "How Do You Taste," 105 (1974): 29.

———. "Why Wives Overeat," 102 (1972).

Science News Letter, "Add Two Pounds Daily," 83 (1963):403.

————. "Body Changes in Fasting," 66 (1946):5.

————. "To Reduce, Fast 10 Days," 82 (1962):4.

Seeger, Murray. "Soviet Cure-All: Eat Nothing for 30 Days," *Los Angeles Times,* April 3, 1972.

Senior, Boris. Editor's Column, *Journal of Pediatrics* 82, no. 3 (1973):555.

Shabad, Theodore. "Russians Advised to Eat 4 Meals a Day," *New York Times,* June 12, 1972.

Shelton, Herbert M. *Facts About Fasting,* Ahimsa Booklet no. 4 (1972).

————. *Fasting Can Save Your Life* (Chicago: Natural Hygiene Press, 1964).

————. *Fasting for Renewal of Life* (Chicago: Natural Hygiene Press, 1974).

Shepard, Richard F., "For the Stylishly Stout, Portly or Just Fat, Life is Not Easy," *The New York Times,* March 3, 1975.

Sherrill, James W. "A Study in Fasting," *Cyclopedia of Medicine* 5 (1932):626–63.

Shigematsu, M. Letter to Jerome Agel, June 5, 1974.

Simonson, Ernst, et al. "The Effect of Meals on the Electrocardiogram in Normal Subjects," *American Heart Journal* 32 (1946):202–14.

Sinclair, Upton. *The Fasting Cure* (Pasadena, Calif.: Sinclair, 1923).

————. "Fasting—the Foe of Sickness," *Cosmopolitan* 50 (1910–11):328–36.

————. "Starving for Health's Sake," *Cosmopolitan* 48 (1910): 739–46.

Sletten, Ivan W., et al. "Total Fasting in Psychiatric Subjects: Psychological, Physiological and Biochemical Changes," *Canadian Psychiatric Association Journal* 12, no. 6 (1967): 553–58.

Snider, Arthur J. "A Fast Way to Lose Weight," *Chicago Daily News Syndicate,* Oct. 1975.

————."Nature Fights Starvation," *Science Digest,* May 1972: 48–49.

————. "The Progress of Medicine," *Science Digest,* Oct. 1963: 52–53.

————. "The Woman Who Stopped Eating," *Science Digest,* April 1964: 81–83.

Snyder, Camilla. "Gayelord Hauser: On the Move at 80," *New York Times,* March 24, 1974.

Spencer, Herta, et al. "Changes in Metabolism in Obese Persons During Starvation," *American Journal of Medicine* 40 (1966):27–37.

Spencer, I. O. B. "Death During Therapeutic Starvation for Obesity," *Lancet* i (1968):1288–90.

Stahel, Thomas H., S.J. "When You Fast, Do Not Look Dismal," *America*, March 2, 1974: 161.

Stein, Marjorie. "Dieting to Disaster," *Mademoiselle*, Jan. 1974.

Stewart, William K. and Fleming, Laura W. Letter to the Editor, *Lancet*, June 7, 1969.

———. "Relationship Between Plasma and Erythrocyte Magnesium and Potassium Concentrations in Fasting Obese Subjects, *Metabolism: Clinical and Experimental* 22, no. 4 (1973.)

Stunkard, Albert and McLaren-Hume, Mavis. "The Results of Treatment for Obesity," *Archives of Internal Medicine* 103, no. 1 (1959).

Sullivan, Walter. "Monsoon Shift Called Threat to World Food," *New York Times*, Jan. 26, 1974.

Susskind, Charles. *Understanding Technology* (Baltimore: Johns Hopkins University Press, 1973).

Swanson, David W. and Dinello, Frank A. "Follow-up of Patients Starved for Obesity," *Psychosomatic Medicine* 32, no. 2 (1970):209–14.

———. "Severe Obesity as a Habituation Syndrome: Evidence During a Starvation Study," *Archives of General Psychiatry* 22, no. 2 (1970):120–27.

Swendseid, Marian E., et al. "Nitrogen and Weight Losses During Starvation and Realimentation in Obesity," *Journal of the American Dietetic Association* 46 (1965):276–79.

Tallmer, Jerry. "At Home with Lady Jean Campbell," *New York Post*, April 8, 1972.

Taub, Harold J. "Eat Less to Live More," *Prevention*, Oct. 1973.

Taylor, Henry Longstreet, et al. "The Effect of Successive Fasts on the Ability of Men to Withstand Fasting During Hard Work," *American Journal of Physiology* 143, no. 1 (1945): 148–55.

Teltsch, Kathleen. "Peril to 400 Million Is Seen by UNICEF," *New York Times*, May 14, 1974.

Thomson, T. J., et al. "Treament of Obesity by Total Fasting for Up to 249 Days," *Lancet* ii (1966):992-96.

Thurston, Herbert. "Living Without Eating," *Month* 158 (1931):217–28.

Tiengo, A., et al. "Metabolic and Hormonal Patterns After Three Days of Total Fasting in 27 Obese and Non-Obese Subjects," *Israel Journal of Medical Sciences* 8, 6 (1972): 821–22.

Time. "Fasting Is Not Enough," Dec. 9, 1974: 14.

———. "Fat Faddists, Beware," Dec. 16, 1974: 105–106.

———. "The Return of Fasting," Dec. 16, 1974: 86–87.

———. "Hungry Men," Review of *The Biology of Human Starvation*, by Dr. Ancel Keys, June 12, 1950: 46.

Trecker, Barbara. "The Battle Against Weight," part 5, *New York Post*, Jan. 11, 1974: 35.

U.S. News & World Report. "How Safe Is the Food You Eat?" April 8, 1974: 39–42.

Van Horne, Harriet. "Portents of Doom" and "Farmer Brown: R.I.P.," *New York Post,* 1974.

Van Kuren, Susan. "Doctor Warns of Dangers of Food Additives," *Windsor* (Ont.) *Star,* March 12, 1974.

Verdy, Maurice. "BSP Retention During Total Fasting," *Metabolism: Clinical and Experimental* 15, no. 9 (1966).

————. "Effet de la Renutrition au Glucose Après le Jeûne, sur la Bilirubine et la BSP," *Médicale du Canada* 102 (1973):2514–15.

————. "Fasting in Obese Females," *American Journal of Clinical Nutrition* 23, no. 8 (1970):1033–36.

————. "Fasting in Obese Females: 1. A Study of Thyroid Function Tests, Serum Proteins and Electrolytes," *Canadian Medical Association Journal* 98, no. 22 (1968):1031–33.

Verdy, Maurice and Champlain, Jacques. "Fasting in Obese Females: 2. Plasma Renin Activity and Urinary Aldosterone," *Canadian Medical Association Journal* 98, no. 22 (1968): 1034–37.

Verdy, Maurice and Marc-Aurele, J. "Fasting in Obese Females: Plasma Renin After Glucose Refeeding," *Hormone and Metabolic Research* 5, no. 1 (1973):59.

Village Voice. "Scenes: An Interview with Dr. Allan Cott," Aug. 22, 1974.

Von Hoffman, Nicholas. "Why Be Healthy?" *Prevention,* Feb. 1973: 69.

Wade, Carlson. *The Natural Way to Health Through Controlled Fasting* (New York: Arc Books, 1968).

Walczak, Michael and Huemer, Richard P. *Applied Nutrition in Clinical Practice* (New York: Intercontinental Medical Book Corp., 1973).

Webster, P. D., et al. "Effects of Feeding and Fasting on the Pancreas," *Gastroenterology* 62, no. 4 (1972):600–605.

Weinraub, Bernard. "Lag in Fertilizer Threatens India," *New York Times,* April 4, 1974.

Weinsier, Roland L. "Fasting: A Review with Emphasis on the Electrolytes," *American Journal of Medicine* 50, no. 2 (1971):233–40.

Westermarck, Edward. "The Principles of Fasting," *Folk-Lore* 18, no. 4 (1907):391–422.

Windmueller, H. G. "Elevated Riboflavin Levels in Urine of Fasting Human Subjects," *American Journal of Clinical Nutrition* 15, no. 2 (1964).

Winter, Ruth. "Are you a 'Yo-Yo' Dieter?" *Science Digest,* May 1974: 36–40.

Woodham-Smith, Cecil. *The Great Hunger: Ireland 1845–1849* (New York: Harper & Row, 1962).

——. *Queen Victoria* (New York: Dell, 1974).

Young, Vernon R. and Scrimshaw, Nevin S. "The Physiology of Starvation," *Scientific American* 225, no. 4 (1971): 14–21.

Zborowski, Mark and Herzog, Elizabeth. *Life Is with People: The Culture of the Shtetl* (New York: Schocken Books, 1965).

ABOUT THE AUTHORS

DR. ALLAN COTT is Life Fellow of the American Psychiatric Association, Founding Fellow of the Academy of Orthomolecular Psychiatry and Consultant to the Allan Cott School for children with severe disorders of behavior, communication, and learning—affiliated with the Department of Psychiatry, University of Alabama. He is in private practice in New York City and on the attending staff, Gracie Square Hospital, where he has fasted patients. Dr. Cott has written and lectured on megavitamin treatment in childhood schizophrenia; orthomolecular treatment of learning disabilities and controlled fasting treatment in the Soviet Union.

JEROME AGEL is the author and/or co-author and/or producer of *Herman Kahnsciousness; I Seem To Be a Verb* (with Buckminster Fuller); *The Radical Therapist; Rough Times; The Making of Kubrick's 2001; The Cosmic Connection—An Extraterrestrial Perspective* and *Other Worlds* (with Carl Sagan); *The Medium Is the Massage* (with Marshall McLuhan); *Is Today Tomorrow?—A Synergistic Collage of Alternative Futures; A World Without—What Our Presidents Didn't Know; It's About Time & It's About Time* (with Alan Lakein) and *Understanding Understanding* (with Humphry Osmond).

EUGENE BOE has contributed to many books, including *Cooking Creatively with Natural Foods, The Immigrant Experience, Hart's Guide to New York City, The Wit and Wisdom of Archie Bunker* and *Edith Bunker's All in the Family Cook Book.* His more than two hundred articles have appeared in national magazines.